JAMES MᶜNAIR's
SQUASH
COOKBOOK

Photography by Patricia Brabant
Artworks by Alan May

Chronicle Books • San Francisco

Printed in Hong Kong.

Library of Congress
Cataloging-in-Publication Data
McNair, James K.
[Squash cookbook]
James McNair's squash cookbook
/James McNair;
photography by Patricia Brabant.
artworks by Alan May
p. cm.
Includes index.
ISBN 0-87701-586-4
ISBN 0-87701-579-1 (pbk.)
1. Cookery (Squash) I. Title.
II. Title: Squash cookbook.
TX803.S67M37 1988
641.6'562—dc19   88-36600
                                  CIP

Distributed in Canada by
Raincoast Books
112 East Third Avenue
Vancouver, British Columbia V5T 1C8

10 9 8 7 6 5 4 3 2

Chronicle Books
275 Fifth Street
San Francisco, California 94103

For Stephen Marcus, one of the world's master gardeners, who has generously shared his produce, flowers, recipes, opinions, ideas, family, and loving friendship with me through all my years in San Francisco.

Produced by The Rockpile Press, San Francisco and Lake Tahoe

Art direction, photographic and food styling, and book design by James McNair

Editorial production assistance by Lin Cotton

Photography assistance by Bruce Bennett, Glen Carroll, Carrie Loyd, M.J. Murphy, and Edy Owen

Typography and mechanical production by Cleve Gallat, Don Kruse, and Peter Linato of CTA Graphics

CONTENTS

A DIVERSE FAMILY

Squash are among the home gardener's most prolific crops, the produce vendor's most regularly stocked items, and the imaginative cook's most versatile ingredients. Add the fact that they are inexpensive, low in calories, and high in fiber and nutrition, and you can see why squash deserve a book of their own.

I've divided this volume into two major sections, Summer Squash and Winter Squash. The summer section (pages 9–51) includes the thin-skinned members—'Crookneck,' 'Pattypan,' and 'Zucchini,' as well as their more unusual seasonal cousins—that should be eaten when young and tender, and, preferably, just moments off the vine. They are at their best from late spring into fall, although 'Zucchini' and a few other relatives grown in greenhouses or imported from warmer regions of the continent are available year-round. The winter types (pages 53–93), which develop hard skins as they mature in late summer and in fall, include the acorn-shaped varieties, the tan-skinned 'Butternut,' the odd-shaped 'Hubbard,' and the numerous pumpkins and other squash that signal the advent of autumn.

These pages also demystify the less commonplace members of the family, including the tropical chayote (*Sechium edule*), a longtime ingredient of cooks in Mexico, the Caribbean, and southern Louisiana, and several Asian kin with such descriptive common names as baseball bat squash, fuzzy melon, and bitter melon.

I have gathered my favorite squash recipes here in hope that you will discover new ideas for preparing the bounty of this prolific family. At the same time, you are certain to meet varieties that you will want to introduce to your garden and table. Perhaps you will even be reminded of some forgotten recipes that deserve attention once again.

BOTANICALLY SPEAKING

We usually divide them up as summer squash, winter squash, pumpkins, and edible gourds, but botanically speaking they are all members of the *Cucurbitaceae* family, which also includes cucumbers, melons, and decorative gourds. The majority of our popular summer squash and pumpkins are native to Central America and Mexico, while most of the winter squash, other than pumpkins, originated in the Argentine Andes. Squash of all types were brought north by the Indians.

Amazingly, only three species account for a tremendous number of squash varieties. All of the popular summer squash belong to *Cucurbita Pepo*, which also includes ornamental gourds, the numerous jack-o'-lantern pumpkins, and the 'Acorn' winter squash. Giant prize-winning pumpkins such as 'Big Max,' various types of 'Hubbard' squash, and the very tasty 'Buttercup' are all varieties of the species *C. maxima*. Quite a few of the more flavorful pumpkins and the tan-skinned 'Butternut' are descendants of *C. moschata*.

Extensive crossbreeding has created numerous mixes that blur the distinguishing characteristics of what defines a squash and what defines a pumpkin.

The Home Squash Garden

Squash grow in either bush or vining forms. Bush plants are relatively compact, while vining squash reach out and consume large amounts of the garden and sometimes even nearby lawns and decks. Both forms are easy to grow and prolific; a few plants will provide more squash than most households can use.

Following seed packet directions, sow directly in a well-drained part of the garden or in large pots in a sunny location as early as April in the warmer regions of North America or as late as June in the coldest zones. In cold areas, you can get a jump on the season by starting seeds indoors about 4 weeks before the anticipated last frost date; carefully transplant as soon as all danger of frost is past.

Avoid planting two different varieties too closely together or cross-pollination may produce an unwelcome mix. After sprouting, thin down to a few seedlings, as advised on the seed packet.

During growing season, keep the planting area free of weeds and provide plenty of water for the thirsty squash. Be on the lookout for spoilers such as aphids, striped cucumber beetles, squash beetles, squash borers, squash bugs, and whitefly and attack any infestations promptly. Consult your local nursery personnel for appropriate treatment suggestions. If you must resort to chemical warfare, be sure to scrub or peel the squash thoroughly before using.

A Bountiful Harvest

The blossoms of all squash plants are edible and delicious, whether stuffed, deep fried, sautéed, or added to soups. Small summer squash can be harvested with female flowers still attached for fanciful presentations. Once the swollen base forms on a female blossom, the flower may be carefully cut from the tiny squash, leaving the developing fruit on the vine. It is generally better to harvest the larger male blossoms, those without a swollen base at the stem end; be sure to leave a few males intact to insure necessary pollination. Gather the entire crop of blossoms just before the first frost; cold temperatures curtail fruit production, rendering the flowers useless to the plant.

Expect to pick the first fruits of summer squash plants about 2 months after planting. Harvest them continuously throughout the season; as a general rule, the more you cut, the more you get. Small summer squash are tastier than big ones, so avoid letting the squash grow too large. As the season draws to a close, it may be impossible to eat all the summer squash your garden is producing; some are destined to reach enormous sizes. Large squash with dry flesh serve a better purpose on the compost heap than in the kitchen. On occasion, however, it is fun to transform these big specimens into edible containers for stuffing, as shown on page 42.

Cut squash stems with a sharp knife or pruning shears; don't pull them off or you'll leave open wounds that are breeding grounds for disease.

For optimal flavor, do not harvest winter squash until they are fully mature. The best time is usually after the advent of some cool weather, which enhances their sugar content. When ripe, most winter varieties take on some autumnal coloring and their stems soften or discolor.

SUMMER SQUASH

If you think of summer squash only in terms of the three hues that fill most grocery bins—dark green 'Zucchini,' pale green 'Pattypan,' and light yellow 'Crookneck'—there are many undiscovered treats in store as you explore local farmers' markets, ethnic groceries, and seed catalogs. In recent years, new varieties of these venerable favorites have expanded the offerings.

Consumer demand has also increased the appearance of some of the more unusual native American plants as well as that of exotics. Today most supermarkets carry chayote, a tropical squash that has long been favored in the kitchens of Mexico, the Caribbean, and southern Louisiana. And West Coast supermarkets and Asian specialty grocers feature several squash that originated in the Orient but are now cultivated on this continent.

Some of my favorite summer squash are described on the following two pages. With the exception of the Asian bitter melon, they can be used interchangeably in any recipe calling for summer squash.

SUMMER SQUASH NUTRITION

With only 25 calories per 8-ounce serving, summer squash should be on every dieter's menu. They are also very high in natural fiber, are good sources of vitamins A and C, niacin, riboflavin, and thiamine, and contain some iron, calcium, and potassium.

THE NATIVES

CHAYOTE (*Sechium edule*). Delicately flavored pale green squash from the tropics of Mexico and Central America, also known as vegetable pear (due to its shape), christophine, custard marrow, mango squash, one-seeded cucumber, and in Louisiana as mirliton (sometimes spelled merliton). The single large edible seed, or pit, is a good addition to salads. Although the skin is edible, it is usually pared away; wear rubber gloves when peeling to prevent skin irritation from strong enzymes.

CROOKNECK (*Cucurbita Pepo* 'Summer Crookneck'). This mild-flavored favorite has very thin, often bumpy yellow skin and a narrow curved neck that gives the squash its common name. Look for hybrids in white, light green, or pale gray.

PATTYPAN (*C. Pepo* 'Bush Scallop'). Round, scallop-edged squash, also commonly called cymling, scallop, or bush squash. Don't stop with the pale green pattypans of grocery bins; include white, yellow, or striped varieties.

SCALLOPINI (*C. Pepo* 'Scallopini'). A cross that carries the dark green color of its 'Zucchini' parent and the flying-saucer shape of its 'Pattypan' parent, though thicker from blossom end to stem. 'Sunburst' is a notable cultivar with golden yellow skin and a center splash of deep green.

STRAIGHTNECK (*C. Pepo* 'Summer Straightneck'). Yellow squash reminiscent in flavor to 'Crookneck,' but smooth-skinned and shaped like 'Zucchini.'

ZUCCHINI (*C. Pepo* 'Zucchini'). This most popular of the summer squash is no longer confined to the ubiquitous native American green variety that was transported centuries ago to the Mediterranean where it acclimated so well that we now use the Italian name for it. Known to the French as *courgette*, the mildly flavored squash has been bred to produce shades of gold and gray, and a green so dark it's sold as "black zucchini." In addition to the familiar cylindrical shape, crossbreeding has produced the round 'Globe Zucchini.' With plant hybridizers hard at work, who knows what offspring will be featured in next season's garden catalogs?

THE ASIANS

BASEBALL BAT (*Benincasa hispida*). Looks are what gave this mild-flavored squash its whimsical moniker. Known to the Chinese as *poo gwa*, this edible wax gourd is eaten when about 2 feet long.

BITTER MELON (*Momordica charantia*). As the name implies, this squash has an interestingly bitter taste that some compare to Scotch whisky. The skin is bright green, ridged, and wrinkled.

CALABASH (*Lagenaria siceraria*). An edible bottle-shaped gourd that has all the characteristics of a summer squash when picked young. Mature specimens are dried and used ornamentally or for utilitarian purposes such as bowls or ladles.

FUZZY MELON (*B. hispida*). A delicately sweet wax gourd with a fine hairy coating when young. Edible when immature, up to about 6 inches long. Known in Cantonese as *mo gwa*, the squash comes in two forms, cylindrical and globular. Peel before cooking.

LUFFA GOURD (*Luffa acutangula*). Also called angled luffa, Chinese okra, or *cee gwa*, this Asian native must be harvested and cooked when young and tender; when it matures it is dried, like its cousin *L. cylindrica*, into the long fibrous sponges sold in bath shops. Before slicing into sunburst-shaped rounds, cut off the hard spines, then scrape lightly as you would a carrot.

Preparing Summer Squash
for Cooking

CHOOSING SUMMER SQUASH

Whether cutting from your own plants or purchasing at the market, the first thing to look for when selecting squash is size. Less is usually more, as smaller squash are more flavorful and tender. 'Zucchini' and other long varieties are best when young, from 3 to 5 inches in length; avoid those over 8 inches. Scalloped and round squash are also most desirable when young, preferably under 3 inches in diameter; forgo any that reach much beyond that size. In either case, use larger squash only if you plan to stuff them or use them in soups.

No matter what the size, the skin should be unblemished, brightly colored, and shiny; pass up any that are wrinkled or withered. Next, hold the squash and gently squeeze to be sure it is firm, has no soft spots, and feels heavy and full of moisture; skip those that feel dried out and light in comparison to size. The skin of tender summer squash can be easily punctured with a fingernail, but please don't try this test with those you don't plan to purchase.

Generally, 1 pound of raw summer squash yields about 3 cups sliced, chopped, or grated squash, or enough to serve 4 people.

Always thoroughly wash summer squash under running cold water, rubbing with a soft-bristled scrub brush or kitchen towel to loosen any imbedded soil. Tender young squash may be cooked whole, stems and blossoms attached. Slice off both the stem and blossom ends of larger squash, then cut as directed in recipes.

There is no need to peel or seed most young squash. When you cook older squash or such Asian varieties as fuzzy melon, remove the skin with a vegetable peeler, slice in half lengthwise, and scoop out the seeds with a spoon.

Except in the case of baked goods or soups where you need the high-moisture content, you will want to rid summer squash of excess water that can turn a dish into mush. This can be done by salting or blanching the squash. To salt, slice, grate, or chop the squash as directed in recipes and place in a colander set over a bowl or in a sink. Sprinkle generously with salt, mix with your fingertips to distribute the salt evenly, and let stand for about 30 minutes. If you are on a salt-restricted diet, rinse the squash under running cold water. Gather grated or shredded squash in your hand and gently squeeze to release any additional surface moisture. Pat slices or chunks dry with paper toweling.

To blanch, drop the squash whole or in large pieces into boiling water and cook until the flesh just begins to yield when pressed with your fingertips. Small squash or chunks should cook in 3 to 4 minutes, common grocery-sized squash in 5 to 8 minutes, large whole or halved squash in 8 to 10 minutes, and giant size in 18 to 22 minutes. Start timing after the water returns to a boil. Immediately immerse in ice water to halt cooking and preserve color. Drain well and cool, then use as directed in recipes that call for blanched squash.

Both salting and blanching can be done up to several hours in advance of finishing the dish. Cover and refrigerate until needed.

Cooking Summer Squash

Use the following basic methods to create your own recipes, adding other ingredients, seasonings, or sauces that appeal.

BAKING. As directed on page 12, clean the squash, then shred, chop, or cut into thin slices, bite-sized chunks, or julienne. Salt, drain, and dry squash. Or blanch the cleaned squash as directed, then cut as desired. Arrange in layers in a baking dish, add melted butter or a sauce and selected seasonings, and bake in a preheated 350° F. oven until tender, about 20 to 30 minutes, or a little less for blanched squash.

To prebake summer squash for stuffing, follow the directions on page 34, then fill with your favorite meat, cheese, or vegetable stuffings.

BUTTER-STEAMING. As directed on page 12, clean the squash, then shred, chop, or cut into thin slices, bite-sized chunks, or julienne. Salt, drain, and dry squash. Heat about 3 tablespoons unsalted butter or margarine per 2 cups squash in a pan with a tight-fitting lid over medium-high heat. Stir in the squash and salt, pepper, herbs, and other seasonings to taste, cover, and cook until tender, about 3 to 5 minutes; check often to avoid scorching.

DEEP FRYING. As directed on page 12, clean the squash and cut into strips, rounds, or chunks, or form into balls with a melon-ball scoop. Salt and drain as directed, then soak in ice water for about 30 minutes. Drain and pat dry with paper toweling. Heat at least 3 inches of cooking oil to 370° F. Drop a piece of batter-dipped squash into the oil to test the temperature; the squash should turn golden within about 30 seconds. Add squash pieces, being careful not to crowd the pan. Fry until golden brown, remove with a slotted spoon or fry basket, and drain briefly on paper toweling. Season to taste with salt and pepper.

STORING SUMMER SQUASH

Use summer squash as quickly as possible after harvesting or purchasing. If you must store them, place in a loosely closed plastic bag in the vegetable drawer of a refrigerator for up to 4 days.

Cooked squash can be refrigerated for up to 3 days in a tightly covered container. With the exception of puréed cooked squash, summer squash contains too much water to freeze successfully. To freeze purée, sauté squash in butter with seasonings as desired, purée it, and then freeze in airtight containers or freezer bags; use within a couple of months, preferably for soup, as the moisture content is high.

PURÉEING SUMMER SQUASH

Using any of the cooking methods on pages 13-15 except deep frying, cook squash until very tender, then transfer to a food processor fitted with a steel blade or to a blender and purée until smooth, adding a little of the cooking liquid or some flavorful stock if squash is too dry. With a spatula, scrape down the sides of the container a couple of times during the puréeing.

Use the puréed squash as directed in recipes, or transfer to a saucepan placed over low heat and add a little butter and heavy (whipping) cream, light cream (or half and half), flavorful stock, white sauce, sour cream, or crème fraîche to create a smooth purée. Season to taste with minced fresh herbs or garlic, freshly squeezed lemon juice, freshly grated nutmeg, curry powder, ground ginger or mace, or other favorite seasonings.

As a general rule, 1 pound of raw summer squash yields 1 to 1½ cups of cooked purée.

GRILLING. Grill very small squash whole; slice or halve larger ones. As directed on page 12, clean the squash, then salt, drain, and dry. Or blanch the cleaned squash as directed, then slice or halve, if necessary. Brush all sides with olive oil and cook over a moderate fire until just tender, turning once, about 4 to 5 minutes total. Serve plain or with garlicky *aïoli* sauce, pesto, fresh salsa, or melted butter, herb flavored or plain.

MICROWAVING. As directed on page 12, clean the squash, then shred, chop, or cut into thin slices, bite-sized chunks, or julienne. Salt, drain, and dry squash. Or blanch the cleaned squash as directed, and then cut as desired. Arrange in a microwave dish. For each pound of cleaned whole squash or every 3 cups of cut-up squash, add about 3 tablespoons water and season to taste with salt, pepper, herbs, and other seasonings, if desired. Cover with plastic wrap or a microwave lid and cook on high until tender, about 4 to 5 minutes; turn the dish a quarter turn about halfway through the cooking.

SAUTÉING. As directed on page 12, clean the squash, then shred, chop, or cut into thin slices, bite-sized chunks, or julienne. Salt, drain, and dry squash. Or blanch the cleaned squash as directed, and then cut as desired. For each 3 cups squash, heat about 3 tablespoons unsalted butter, margarine, or oil in a sauté pan or skillet over medium-high heat. Sauté chopped onion, shallots, or garlic until softened, if desired, then add the squash and sauté for a couple of minutes. Reduce the heat to low, cover the pan, and continue to cook, stirring frequently, until the squash is done to your liking. Most sautéed squash can be prepared ahead of time and quickly reheated just before serving.

Chopped tomatoes, fresh corn kernels, herbs, and other seasonings can be added along with the squash.

STEAMING. It is not necessary to salt or blanch squash to remove excess moisture before steaming; the liquid drains away in the cooking. Place whole cleaned squash directly on a steamer rack set over boiling water, cover, and steam until tender, approximately 5 minutes for baby squash, 6 minutes for 3-ounce scalloped varieties or 5-ounce 'Crookneck', or up to 15 minutes for 8-inch 'Zucchini.' Serve baby squash whole; slice or cut larger squash into chunks. Toss with melted butter, freshly squeezed lemon juice, and minced herbs, or a favorite sauce.

Stuffed squash can also be steamed. 'Zucchini' does not require precooking; just prepare and fill as directed in recipes, then steam as above until the squash is tender and the filling is hot. Scalloped or globular varieties should be partially cooked over steam before stuffing, then stuffed and steamed until the squash is tender and the filling is hot.

STIR-FRYING. As directed on page 12, clean the squash, then shred, chop, or cut into thin slices or bite-sized chunks of uniform size. Salt, drain, and dry squash. Or blanch the cleaned squash as directed, then cut as desired. For each 3 cups squash, heat about 2 tablespoons high-quality vegetable oil in a wok or sauté pan placed over high heat. Add the squash and stir-fry until crisp-tender, about 2 to 3 minutes. Season to taste with soy sauce, preferably tamari, or other favorite flavorings.

NO COOKING REQUIRED

'Zucchini' is usually the choice for serving raw, although most other varieties are equally flavorful. Avoid serving the strongly flavored Asian bitter melon squash raw.

Cut summer squash into sticks, cubes, or disks. Arrange attractively on a platter alongside your favorite dip.

To pass on a tray, salt, drain, and pat dry ¼-inch-thick slices of summer squash and top with herbed cream cheese, blue cheese blended with chopped toasted walnuts, or other favorite spread. Garnish with a fresh herb sprig or tiny edible flower.

For an *antipasto*, marinate squash cubes or slices in your favorite Italian-style salad dressing for several hours.

Hollow out large summer squash and fill with summer salads, cold soups, dip for crudités, or even cut flowers.

Use shredded summer squash instead of cabbage in slaw, or add it to potato, pasta, meat, fish, or vegetable salads.

Add thin slices of summer squash to a sandwich for a crisp bite.

Sprinkle chopped squash on gazpacho or other cold soups.

Fried Stuffed Squash Blossoms

This gardening-season treat is great as an appetizer or as an accompaniment to grilled or roasted meats or fish. Be sure to read about harvesting flowers on page 7 before heading into the garden. Look for blossoms for sale in natural-foods stores and specialty produce markets.

If you prefer the flavor of cooked garlic, sauté it briefly in a little butter or olive oil before adding it to the stuffing mixture.

Quickly rinse the squash blossoms under running cold water. Gently pat dry with paper toweling. Cut off and discard the stems. Set aside.

In a bowl, combine the ricotta cheese, garlic, pine nuts, basil, and salt and pepper to taste. Open up the blossoms and spoon about 1½ teaspoons of the mixture into the center of each, avoiding overfilling. Twist the top of each blossom together to close. Place on a baking sheet and refrigerate for about 15 minutes.

Combine the flour and water in a shallow bowl and beat with a small wire whisk until smooth and creamy. Let stand for about 15 minutes.

Pour the oil into a deep skillet or saucepan to a depth of 3/4 inch. Heat over high heat until a small cube of bread dropped into the oil turns golden brown within seconds. Briefly dip each stuffed blossom into the batter, then carefully slip into the hot oil. Cook until golden brown on one side; turn and continue to cook until golden on all sides, about 3 minutes total cooking time. Add only as many blossoms at a time as will fit comfortably in the pan. Transfer with a slotted utensil to paper toweling to drain briefly. Sprinkle with salt and Parmesan cheese to taste and serve immediately.

Serves 4 to 6.

16 large squash blossoms
¼ cup ricotta cheese
1 garlic clove, minced or pressed
1 tablespoon pine nuts
2 tablespoons minced fresh basil
Salt
Freshly ground black pepper
⅔ cup sifted unbleached all-purpose
    flour
1 cup cold water
Safflower or other high-quality
    vegetable oil for frying
Freshly grated Parmesan cheese,
    preferably Parmigiano-Reggiano

Stuffed Baby Squash Appetizers

18 baby summer squash, about 1 to 2
  inches in diameter for round
  types, or about 3 inches long
  for cylindrical types
About 2 tablespoons unsalted butter,
  melted
1 tablespoon unsalted butter
6 ounces cream cheese or very mild
  goat's cheese, softened
⅓ cup unseasoned fine fresh bread
  crumbs, preferably from French
  bread
3 tablespoons minced fresh herbs
  such as basil, chervil, chives,
  parsley, or tarragon
1 tablespoon freshly squeezed
  lemon juice
Salt
Freshly ground black pepper or
  ground cayenne pepper
⅓ cup freshly grated Parmesan cheese,
  preferably Parmigiano-Reggiano
Fresh herb sprigs, same as used
  in filling
Tiny pesticide-free edible flowers
  such as borage, wild garlic, or
  violas for garnish

Here's a recipe to serve as a guide for making appetizers with tiny 'Pattypan,' 'Zucchini,' or other native American summer squash varieties. Use the same technique with any favorite meat, bread, or vegetable stuffing. Whatever filling you choose, keep the seasonings subtle to show off the delicate, garden-fresh character of the young squash.

If necessary, trim squash bottoms so that the squash will stand upright. Drop the squash into boiling salted water and blanch until barely tender, 2 to 3 minutes. Place immediately in ice water to stop the cooking. Drain well and blot dry with paper toweling. Cut away and discard the stem portion of each round squash, or horizontally cut off a thin slice from one side of cylindrical squash. With a tiny spoon, remove the pulp from inside the squash, leaving about a 1/4-inch wall all around. Chop the removed pulp (including the slice from cylindrical squash) and reserve. Brush the insides of the hollowed-out squash with melted butter. Set aside.

Preheat an oven to 350° F.

Melt 1 tablespoon butter in a skillet over medium-high heat, add the chopped pulp, and sauté until tender, mashing it with the back of a spoon as it cooks. Transfer to a bowl and add the cream or goat's cheese, bread crumbs, minced herbs, lemon juice, and salt and pepper to taste. Stir to combine thoroughly. Using a small spoon, stuff the mixture into the squash cavities. Place stuffed squash on a baking sheet, sprinkle the Parmesan cheese over the filling, and pour water to a depth of about ¼ inch over the bottom of the baking sheet. Bake until the squash is heated through and the cheese melts, about 10 minutes. Cool slightly.

Just before serving, garnish each squash with an herb sprig or flower, arrange on a tray, and serve warm or at room temperature.

Serves 6.

Squash Sandwiches

This is a good way to utilize any outsized squash. Serve as an appetizer, snack, or side dish.

Discard stem and blossom ends from the squash and cut into about 16 slices about ½ inch thick; if using cylindrical squash, cut on the diagonal for larger pieces.

Arrange the squash slices in a single layer on paper toweling, sprinkle generously with salt, cover with more paper toweling, and top with a weight. Let stand for 30 minutes. With dry paper toweling, pat off liquid and excess salt. (If desired, rinse off salt and pat dry with paper toweling.)

Lay half of the slices on a flat surface. Top each with a bit of cheese, chopped tomato, and prosciutto or ham. Cover with the remaining squash slices. Dip each sandwich into the beaten egg, then dredge in the bread crumbs, pressing coating on firmly with fingertips and covering all surfaces completely. Place on a baking sheet lined with parchment paper or waxed paper and refrigerate for at least 15 minutes or for up to 1 hour.

In a large sauté pan or skillet, pour olive oil to a depth of 1 inch. Heat over medium-high heat. Add the stuffed squash slices, a few at a time (avoid crowding), and fry on one side until golden. Carefully turn and fry until golden on the second side, about 5 minutes total cooking time. Drain briefly on paper toweling and sprinkle with salt and Parmesan to taste. Serve warm or at room temperature.

Serves 4 to 6.

1½ to 2 pounds large summer squash
Salt
½ cup (about 2½ ounces) shredded Bel Paese, Fontina, or other good-melting Italian cheese
1½ tablespoons chopped sun-dried tomato
2 ounces prosciutto or other flavorful ham, thinly sliced and then chopped or slivered
2 eggs, beaten
½ unseasoned fine dry bread crumbs, preferably from French or Italian bread
Olive oil for panfrying
Freshly grated Parmesan cheese, preferably Parmigiano-Reggiano

Summer Squash Soup

3 tablespoons unsalted butter or
  olive oil
¼ cup minced shallot, or 1 cup
  chopped leek, white portion only
  if making yellow soup
2 teaspoons minced or pressed garlic
10 cups (about 3 pounds) stemmed
  and coarsely chopped yellow
  or green summer squash
About 1 quart homemade vegetable
  or chicken stock or canned
  chicken broth
½ cup heavy (whipping) cream, light
  cream, or half and half
Salt
Freshly ground black or white pepper
Soy sauce, preferably tamari
  (optional)
Pesticide-free edible flowers such
  as borage, nasturtium, or squash
  blossoms for garnish (optional)
Whole or snipped chives for garnish

Create a festive presentation by preparing two batches of this soup—
one made with a yellow squash such as 'Gold Rush' zucchini or the
brightly hued scalloped 'Sunburst' scallopini, and the other with a
green summer squash. Serve together in bowls by pouring from two
equally filled ladles simultaneously; if desired, draw a wooden skewer
through the top of the soup to create a swirled pattern.

In a saucepan, heat the butter or oil over medium-low heat. Add the shallot
or leek, cover, and cook until soft, about 10 minutes. Stir in the garlic and
sauté 1 minute longer. Add the squash, cover, reduce the heat to low, and
cook for 8 minutes. Remove the cover, stir in enough chicken stock or broth
to cover barely, bring to a boil, reduce the heat to low, and simmer until
the squash is tender, about 15 minutes.

Working in batches, transfer squash mixture to a food processor or blender
and purée until smooth. Pour into a clean saucepan, stir in the cream, and
season to taste with salt, pepper, and soy sauce, if using. Place over medium-
low heat to heat through, about 4 minutes; do not boil. Ladle into warmed
soup bowls and garnish with blossoms, if using, and chives.

Serves 6.

VARIATIONS: For a squash and tomato bisque, reduce the squash to
5 cups and sauté squash with 5 cups peeled, seeded, and chopped ripe
tomatoes. If available, use yellow tomato varieties with yellow squash.
If you like spicy foods, sauté some minced fresh chili pepper along with the
squash, or add high-quality curry powder to taste to the melted butter.

Substitute 2 cups dry white wine for 2 cups of the stock.

For a tangy calorie-saving version, substitute plain low-fat yogurt for
the cream.

Southeast Asian Squash Soup

Choose a squash favored in the Orient such as fuzzy melon, baseball bat squash, or tender young luffa (page 11) for making this spicy yet soothing soup. Chayote (page 10) or any of the other native American summer varieties will also work well.

For a smooth soup, cook squash in stock until tender, transfer in batches to a food processor or blender, and purée until smooth. Pour into a clean saucepan, add coconut milk, and complete as directed. The soup may be chilled and served cold; taste and adjust seasonings after chilling.

If using fuzzy melon, peel the squash. If using luffa, cut off the tips of the spiny ridges and gently scrape the peel. Slice about ½ inch thick or cut into ½-inch cubes. Reserve.

Heat the oil in a large saucepan over medium-high heat. Add the shallot or onion and chili pepper and sauté until soft, about 5 minutes. Add the garlic, ground coriander, cumin, and turmeric and sauté 1 minute longer. Add the reserved squash and sauté briefly to coat the squash pieces well. Add the chicken stock or broth and bring to a boil. Cover, reduce the heat to low, and simmer until the squash is tender, about 20 to 25 minutes.

Add the coconut milk, fish or soy sauce, lime juice, and salt and pepper to taste. Place over medium heat until heated through. Ladle into heated bowls and garnish with lime slices and cilantro.

Serves 4.

NOTE: If you cannot locate canned coconut milk in markets that specialize in Asian foods, cover 4 cups fresh or dried unsweetened (dessicated) grated coconut with 6 cups boiling water or warmed milk and let stand for 30 minutes. Strain the liquid through cheesecloth, squeezing cloth to extract all the liquid.

1½ pounds summer squash, preferably an Asian variety
2 tablespoons safflower or other high-quality vegetable oil
¾ cup minced shallot or yellow onion
1 to 2 tablespoons minced fresh hot green or red chili pepper
1 teaspoon minced or pressed garlic
2 teaspoons ground coriander
1 teaspoon ground cumin
½ teaspoon ground turmeric
2½ cups homemade chicken stock or canned chicken broth
2 cups canned unsweetened coconut milk (see note)
2 tablespoons fish sauce (available in Asian markets), or 1 tablespoon soy sauce
¼ cup freshly squeezed lime juice
Salt
Freshly ground black pepper
Lime slices for garnish
Chopped fresh cilantro (coriander) for garnish

Summer Garden Matchstick Salad

3 tablespoons freshly squeezed lemon
juice or white-wine vinegar, or to
taste
½ cup olive oil, preferably extra-
virgin
1 teaspoon Dijon-style mustard
1 tablespoon minced fresh chives
2 teaspoons minced fresh parsley,
summer savory, tarragon, or
other herb of choice
Salt
Freshly ground black pepper
2 3-inch-long 'Zucchini' or other
summer squash, cut into julienne
1 medium-sized carrot, cut into
julienne
½ large red or golden sweet pepper,
cut into julienne
1 medium-sized leek, including some
of the green tops, cut into
julienne

For an elegant salad course, bundle individual servings of this colorful
mélange in lettuce leaves and tie each packet with a whole chive that
has been softened by dipping briefly in boiling water. This simple
garden-fresh mixture also makes a perfect light lunch along with some
crusty bread.

In a small bowl, combine the lemon juice or vinegar, olive oil, mustard,
chives, parsley or other herb, and salt and pepper to taste and whisk to
blend well. Reserve.

In a large bowl, combine the squash, carrot, pepper, and leek. Add the
reserved dressing to taste and toss well.

Serves 4 to 6.

Fried Summer Squash and Lemon Slices

Malt vinegar and crushed hot chili pepper add a tangy edge to crisply fried squash pieces. In place of the beer batter, dip the squash pieces in flour, then beaten egg, and finally fine dry bread crumbs; or in a mixture of equal parts cornmeal and flour.

In a bowl, combine the flour, salt, egg yolks, beer, and butter and beat until smooth. Let stand at room temperature for about 1 hour.

Cut the squash into sticks about the size of french-fried potatoes or into disks about ½ inch in diameter. Alternatively, use a melon-ball scoop to form rounds from larger squash. Place squash pieces in a colander set over a bowl or in the sink, sprinkle with salt, and let stand for about 30 minutes. Pat dry with paper toweling.

Pour oil in a deep fryer or saucepan to a depth of about 3 inches. Heat to 360° F., or until a small piece of bread dropped into the oil browns within a few seconds.

Dip squash pieces and lemon slices into the batter, drop into the hot oil, and fry, turning frequently with a slotted spoon or tongs, until they are golden brown and crusty, about 3 to 5 minutes total cooking time. Cook in batches, without overcrowding. Remove with a slotted utensil and drain on paper toweling. Sprinkle with salt, malt vinegar, and chili pepper flakes to taste. Serve hot.

Serves 4.

1 cup unbleached all-purpose flour
1 teaspoon salt
2 egg yolks, beaten
¾ cup beer
3 tablespoons unsalted butter, melted
1 pound 'Zucchini' or other summer
    squash
Salt
High-quality vegetable oil for deep
    frying
2 lemons, thinly sliced and seeded
Malt vinegar
Crushed dried hot chili pepper

Summer Squash Timbale

This recipe was shared by Linda Claasen, chef at the Hotel Carter in Eureka, California. She grows a wide variety of herbs in her flourishing garden plots, allowing her to change the flavor of these delicious timbales continuously.

Place the squash in a colander set over a bowl or in a sink, generously sprinkle with salt, mix with fingertips to distribute salt evenly, and let stand for 30 minutes. Gather squash in your hand and gently squeeze to release any additional surface moisture. Reserve.

Heat the olive oil in a sauté pan or skillet over medium-high heat. Add the onion and sauté until soft, about 5 minutes. Add the garlic and sauté 1 minute longer. Remove from the heat, toss with the squash, and stir in the minced herbs. Add the beaten eggs and cream and season to taste with salt and pepper.

Preheat an oven to 350° F.

Butter the bottom and sides of a 5-cup mold or 10 ½-cup metal timbale molds or ceramic custard cups. Dust mold(s) with bread crumbs to coat completely; shake out excess crumbs. Fill the crumb-lined container(s) with the squash mixture. Transfer to a deep baking pan and add hot water to reach two-thirds up the sides of the timbale(s). Bake, uncovered, until set, about 1 hour for a large mold, or about 30 minutes for small ones. Remove from the oven and let stand about 5 minutes, then run a thin-bladed knife or rubber spatula around the inside edge of the mold(s) and invert onto a platter or individual serving plates. Sprinkle with Parmesan cheese and garnish with fresh herb sprigs.

Serves 8 to 10 as a side dish.

4 cups (about 1⅓ pounds) grated
    or finely chopped young summer
    squash
Salt
2 tablespoons olive oil, preferably
    extra-virgin
1 cup finely chopped yellow onion
1 teaspoon minced or pressed garlic,
    or to taste
3 tablespoons minced fresh herbs such
    as basil, chives, marjoram,
    parsley, and savory, alone or
    in combination
5 eggs, beaten
2 cups heavy (whipping) cream
Salt
Freshly ground black pepper
Butter for greasing mold(s)
About 1 cup unseasoned fine dry
    bread crumbs, preferably from
    French bread
Freshly grated Parmesan cheese,
    preferably Parmigiano-Reggiano
Fresh herb sprigs, same as used in
    the timbales, for garnish

Zucchini, Leek, and Chèvre Tart in Wild Rice Crust

WILD RICE CRUST
1 egg
⅓ cup freshly grated Parmesan cheese,
    preferably Parmigiano-Reggiano
2 tablespoons freshly squeezed
    lemon juice
3 tablespoons unsalted butter,
    melted
2½ cups cooked wild rice
Salt
Freshly ground black pepper

CUSTARD FILLING
2 cups (about 10 ounces) finely
    chopped or coarsely shredded
    'Zucchini' or other summer
    squash
Salt
¼ pound (1 stick) unsalted butter
2 cups thinly sliced leek, including
    some of the green tops
4 eggs
1½ cups heavy (whipping) cream
1 teaspoon Dijon-style mustard
1 cup crumbled chèvre (goat's milk)
    cheese
1 tablespoon chopped fresh marjoram
    or savory, or 1 teaspoon crumbled
    dried marjoram
Freshly ground black pepper

Crunchy wild rice is a satisfying counterpoint to the creamy French custard filling. Cooked brown or white rice can be substituted for a more subtle flavor.

To prepare the mound of crispy topping shown here, very finely shred about 1 pound 'Zucchini,' then follow directions on page 13 for deep frying. A few minutes before the tart comes out of the oven, fry the chilled squash in olive oil, drain briefly on paper toweling, pile on top of the warm tart, and serve immediately.

Preheat an oven to 350° F.

To make the crust, beat the egg, cheese, lemon juice, and melted butter together in a bowl. Stir in the cooked rice, season to taste with salt and pepper, transfer to a 9-inch pie pan, and press with your fingertips to cover bottom and sides evenly. Bake until set and crisp, about 15 minutes. Remove from the oven and cool to room temperature, about 30 minutes. (Or cover and refrigerate as long as overnight; return to room temperature before filling.)

Meanwhile, make the filling. Place the squash in a colander set over a bowl or in a sink. Generously sprinkle with salt, mix with your fingertips to distribute the salt, and let stand for 30 minutes. Gather squash in your hand and gently squeeze to release any additional surface moisture. Reserve.

Heat the butter in a sauté pan or skillet over medium-high heat, add the leek, and sauté until soft, about 5 minutes. Add the drained squash and sauté about 5 minutes longer; reserve.

In a bowl, combine the eggs, cream, mustard, cheese, marjoram, and salt and pepper to taste and whisk to blend well. Stir in the leek and squash mixture, pour into the rice shell, and bake in the 350° F. oven until filling is set and the top is golden, about 30 to 35 minutes. Serve hot or at room temperature.

Serves 6.

Herbed Summer Squash Purée

1 pound new or boiling potatoes
3 tablespoons unsalted butter, melted
½ cup heavy (whipping) cream
2 tablespoons olive oil, preferably
    extra-virgin
½ cup finely chopped yellow onion
3 cups (about 1 pound) chopped
    summer squash
1 teaspoon minced or pressed garlic,
    or to taste
2 tablespoons minced fresh parsley,
    preferably flat-leaf type
1 tablespoon minced fresh chives
1 teaspoon minced fresh sage
1 teaspoon minced fresh thyme
Salt
Freshly ground black pepper
Fresh herb sprigs for garnish
Pesticide-free edible flowers such as
    violas, borage, or nasturtium
    for garnish

Fresh herbs are critical to the success of this dish. If they are unavailable, prepare a different recipe.

To serve the purée in a fanciful manner, cut off and reserve the tops of 6 small squash. With a small spoon or melon-ball scoop, remove the pulp from the squash, leaving a shell about ¼ inch thick; use pulp as part of the chopped squash called for in the ingredients. Rub the shells and tops, inside and out, with olive oil and season to taste with salt, pepper, and minced garlic, if desired. Place the shells and the tops in a baking dish and cook, covered, at 325° F. until the squash are tender but still hold their shape, about 20 minutes. Fill each baked shell with a portion of the warm squash purée, add the tops, and serve immediately.

Place the potatoes in a saucepan and add water to cover. Bring to a boil over medium-high heat and cook until tender when pierced, about 15 to 20 minutes; drain and reserve cooking liquid. Cool potatoes slightly, then peel off and discard skins. Transfer to a bowl and mash with a potato masher or put through a ricer. Stir in the butter and cream and beat with a wire whisk until smooth and silky, adding reserved cooking liquid, a little at a time, if the potatoes seem dry. Reserve.

Heat the olive oil in a sauté pan or skillet over medium-high heat. Add the onion and sauté until soft, about 5 minutes. Add the squash and sauté until very tender, about 10 minutes longer. Stir in the garlic and sauté 1 minute longer. Transfer to a food processor or blender and purée until fairly smooth. Transfer to the bowl containing the potato purée and add the parsley, chives, sage, and thyme. Whisk to blend well, then season to taste with salt and pepper.

Serve the purée in a bowl or spoon onto individual plates. For a decorative presentation, press the mixture through a pastry tube fitted with a large fluted tip, or stuff into the shells as described in the introduction. In any case, garnish with herb sprigs and flowers.

Serves 6.

Lemon-Glazed Asian Squash

Asian relatives of our American summer squash are among the most interesting members of the vegetable kingdom. Choose one type or combine several varieties (see page 11) for this basic stir-fry.

In a bowl, combine the cornstarch, water, sherry, lemon juice, soy sauce, sugar, ginger, and lemon zest. Stir to combine; reserve.

Place a wok or sauté pan over high heat. Add the oil and swirl to coat the bottom and sides of the pan. Add the garlic and stir-fry for 1 minute. Add the squash and stir-fry until the squash skin brightens and the slices are crisp-tender. Stir the reserved sauce, add it to the pan, and stir-fry until the sauce thickens and the vegetables are well glazed. Season to taste with salt and hot chili oil, if desired, and serve immediately.

Serves 4 as a side dish.

1 tablespoon cornstarch
1 tablespoon cold water
2 tablespoons dry sherry
2 tablespoons freshly squeezed lemon juice
1 tablespoon soy sauce
2 tablespoons granulated sugar
1 tablespoon peeled and minced fresh ginger root
1 teaspoon grated or minced lemon zest
2 tablespoons safflower or other high-quality vegetable oil
2 garlic cloves, minced or pressed
1 pound Asian squash, peeled, if necessary, and sliced about ⅛ to ¼ inch thick
Salt
Asian-style hot chili oil (optional)

TOMATO SALSA

2 large ripe tomatoes, peeled, seeded, and chopped
1 medium-sized yellow onion, finely chopped
2 garlic cloves, minced or pressed
3 or 4 fresh hot chili peppers, seeded, if desired, and minced
½ cup minced fresh cilantro (coriander)
2 teaspoons freshly squeezed lime juice
Salt

SPICY SQUASH CAKES

4 eggs
4 cups (about 1⅓ pounds) finely chopped or grated summer squash
1 cup fresh corn kernels (cut from about 2 large ears)
¼ cup finely chopped green onion, including some of the green tops
1 tablespoon minced fresh mild to hot chili pepper, seeded if desired, or to taste
⅓ cup freshly grated Parmesan cheese, preferably Parmigiano-Reggiano
1 cup freshly grated sharp Cheddar cheese
½ cup unbleached all-purpose flour
3 tablespoons unsalted butter, melted
Salt
Freshly ground black pepper
Ground cayenne pepper
Safflower or other high-quality vegetable oil for sautéing

Sour cream (optional)
Fresh cilantro (coriander) sprigs for garnish

Spicy Squash Cakes with Tomato Salsa

Control the fieriness of the chili peppers by adjusting the amount and type used. To pass the cakes as appetizers, cook the squash mixture by teaspoonfuls, arrange on a tray, and top each tiny cake with small dollops of salsa and sour cream.

To make the salsa, combine the tomato, onion, garlic, chili pepper, cilantro, lime juice, and salt to taste in a bowl; reserve.

To make the cakes, beat the eggs in a large bowl. Beat in the squash, corn, green onion, chili pepper, Parmesan and Cheddar cheeses, flour, and melted butter. Season to taste with salt and black and cayenne peppers.

Heat about 2 tablespoons oil in a sauté pan or skillet over medium-high heat. Spoon about 2 tablespoons of the squash mixture per cake into the hot oil and flatten to create uniform thickness; do not crowd the pan. Cook until golden brown on the bottom, then turn and cook the other side until golden brown, about 3 minutes total cooking time per cake. Transfer to a dish or pan lined with paper toweling and place in a warm oven. Cook the remaining cakes.

To serve, arrange the cakes on individual plates with some of the salsa and a dollop of sour cream. Garnish with cilantro sprigs.

Serves 6.

Stuffed Chayote

8 medium-sized chayote squash
(about 6 to 8 ounces each)
3 tablespoons safflower or other
high-quality vegetable oil
3 tablespoons unsalted butter
1 cup finely chopped yellow onion
¾ cup finely chopped green onion,
including some of the green tops
½ cup finely chopped red or green
sweet pepper
¼ cup finely chopped celery
1 tablespoon minced or pressed garlic
2 medium-sized tomatoes, peeled
and seeded, if desired,
and chopped
¼ cup minced fresh parsley,
preferably flat-leaf type
1 tablespoon minced fresh thyme
leaves, or 1 teaspoon crumbled
dried thyme
1 bay leaf, finely crumbled
¾ pound raw shrimp, peeled,
deveined, and coarsely chopped
½ pound (about 1 cup) cooked lump
crab meat, picked over
½ cup unseasoned coarse fresh
bread crumbs, preferably from
French bread
Salt
Freshly ground black pepper
Ground cayenne pepper
About 3 tablespoons unsalted butter,
cut into small pieces
Fresh thyme sprigs for garnish
Fresh lemon wedges for garnish

Known in some areas as vegetable pear or christophine, and as mirliton in Louisiana, delicate-tasting chayotes (*Sechium edule*) are superb when stuffed New Orleans Creole style. They're also wonderful sliced, steamed until crisp tender, and dressed, along with their edible single large seed, in a mustard vinaigrette.

Cut off and discard stem end from each squash and slice the vegetable in half lengthwise. Remove seeds and use in another dish, if desired. If necessary, cut a thin slice off the rounded side of each half so it will sit level. Place halves on a steamer rack set over simmering water, cover, and steam until crisp-tender, about 20 to 25 minutes. Or boil in water to cover in a covered pot until tender, about 25 to 30 minutes. Remove from steamer or pot and let stand until cool enough to handle. Using a spoon, scoop out the flesh from each squash half into a bowl, leaving a shell about ¼ inch thick; reserve.

Preheat an oven to 350° F.

To make the stuffing, heat 3 tablespoons each oil and butter in a skillet over medium-high heat. Add the yellow and green onions, sweet pepper, and celery and sauté until the vegetables are soft, about 5 minutes. Add the garlic and sauté 1 minute. Stir in the tomatoes, reserved squash pulp, parsley, minced thyme, and bay leaf and continue to cook until all the vegetables are almost tender, about 5 minutes longer. Reduce the heat to medium-low, stir in the shrimp pieces, and cook until they turn bright pink. Stir in the cooked crab and bread crumbs and season to taste with salt and black and cayenne peppers.

Mound the stuffing mixture into the reserved squash halves. Dot the tops with butter and place in a greased baking dish. Bake until the tops are golden brown, about 25 minutes. Garnish with thyme sprigs and lemon wedges and serve piping hot.

Serves 8.

Meat-Stuffed Giant Summer Squash

Backyard plants often produce more squash than can be eaten while the squash are young and tender. Near summer's end, take advantage of such outsized bounty as the huge 'Golden Zucchini' or 'Pattypan' shown here; at other times, divide the stuffing mixture among a number of smaller squash.

Slice a thin lengthwise layer off a cylindrical squash, or cut off the top of a round squash. Using a spoon, scoop out the pulp, leaving a shell about ½ inch thick. Use pulp in soup or discard if too dry. If necessary cut a thin slice off the base of the squash so it will sit level. Salt the cavity, invert on a wire rack set over a bowl or in a sink, and let stand for about 30 minutes to drain off any excess moisture.

Heat the olive oil in a sauté pan or skillet over medium-high heat. Add the onion and sauté until tender, about 5 minutes. Add the garlic and sauté 1 minute longer. Add the ground pork and beef and sauté meat until just past the pink stage, breaking it up with a wooden spoon as it cooks. Stir in the tomatoes, reduce the heat to medium-low, and simmer until the liquid evaporates, about 10 minutes. Remove from the heat and stir in the bread crumbs, parsley, oregano, and salt and peppers to taste.

Preheat an oven to 350° F.

Pat the squash cavity dry with paper toweling. Fill with the stuffing mixture and place the squash in a baking pan. Add hot water to a depth of about 1 inch and bake until the squash is tender but still holds its shape, about 45 minutes. Sprinkle with Parmesan cheese and serve warm or at room temperature. To serve, cut cylindrical squash into 1-inch-thick slices or cut round squash into wedges.

Serves 4.

1 3- to 4-pound summer squash
3 tablespoons olive oil, preferably extra-virgin
1 cup chopped yellow onion
2 tablespoons minced or pressed garlic
½ pound ground lean pork
½ pound ground lean beef
2 cups peeled, seeded, and chopped ripe or drained canned tomatoes
2 cups unseasoned fine dry bread crumbs
¼ cup minced fresh parsley, preferably flat-leaf type
1 tablespoon minced fresh oregano, or 1 teaspoon crumbled dried oregano
Salt
Freshly ground black pepper
Ground cayenne pepper
Freshly grated Parmesan cheese, preferably Parmigiano-Reggiano

Squash Pickles

Use the same technique as for these bread and butter pickles to pack, process, and store the relish variation.

In a saucepan, combine the vinegar, sugar, salt, celery seed, dill seed, turmeric, and mustard. Bring to a boil over medium-high heat. Mix the squash and onion slices in a ceramic bowl, pour the vinegar mixture over, and let stand at room temperature for 1 hour.

Sterilize jars, lids, rings, and all the utensils in boiling water for 15 minutes. Remove and place upside down on paper toweling.

Transfer the squash mixture to a large pot over medium-high heat. Bring to a boil and cook for 3 minutes. Pack immediately into hot sterilized jars, leaving about ½ inch head room. Wipe jar rim threads clean with paper toweling, cover with lids, and tighten rings. Place jars on a rack in a large pot of enough boiling water to cover the jar tops by at least 2 inches. Return the water to a boil, cover, and let jars stand in the boiling water for 10 minutes. With a jar lifter, lift each jar straight up out of the water bath. Place jars on a counter and let stand undisturbed until cold. Check the seal on the lids after 24 hours; the lids should be slightly depressed. Store any jars that did not seal properly in the refrigerator and use contents as soon as possible. Store sealed jars in a cool, dark, dry place for at least a week before eating. Refrigerate after opening.

Makes 6 to 7 pints.

VARIATION: For mixed garden relish, combine 4 cups *each* finely chopped summer squash and grated white onion, 2 cups finely chopped carrot, 1½ cups minced red sweet pepper, ¼ cup minced fresh hot chili pepper, 2½ cups distilled white vinegar (4 to 6 percent acidity), ¼ cup salt, ¾ cup granulated sugar, and 1 tablespoon mustard seed in a saucepan. Bring to a boil over medium-high heat, reduce the heat to low, and simmer for 10 minutes. Pack into jars and process in a boiling water bath as described above, reducing time to 5 minutes.

2 quarts distilled white vinegar of 4 to 6 percent acidity
4 cups granulated sugar
6 tablespoons salt
4 teaspoons celery seed
4 teaspoons dill seed
4 teaspoons ground turmeric
2 teaspoons dry mustard
4 quarts (about 5 pounds) thinly sliced 'Zucchini' or other summer squash
1 quart (about 3 or 4 large) thinly sliced white onion

Orange and Squash Muffins

Delicious for breakfast or afternoon tea spread with whipped unsalted butter mixed with minced orange zest.

Place the squash in a colander set over a bowl or in the sink, sprinkle with about 1 tablespoon of salt, mix with your fingertips, and let stand for 30 minutes. Gently squeeze to release moisture and pat dry with paper toweling; reserve.

Preheat an oven to 350° F. Grease 12 regular-sized muffin-tin wells.

Beat the eggs in a mixing bowl until lemon colored. Add the sugar, oil, orange juice and zest, and vanilla. Beat until thick and smooth.

In a separate bowl, combine the flour, baking powder, baking soda, ½ teaspoon salt, nutmeg, and cinnamon. Fold the dry mixture into the egg mixture, stirring just until well blended. Fold in the drained zucchini and the raisins. Spoon batter into the prepared muffin-tin wells, filling each about three-fourths full, and sprinkle the sugar-nutmeg mixture over the top. Bake until a wooden skewer inserted in the center of a muffin tests clean, about 20 to 25 minutes. Cool in the muffin tins for about 3 minutes before turning out. Serve warm.

Makes about 12 muffins; serves 6 to 8.

VARIATION: To bake as a loaf, pour the batter into a greased 9-by-5-inch loaf pan and bake for about 1 hour. Cool in the pan for 10 minutes before turning out.

1 cup (about 5 ounces) shredded or finely chopped summer squash
Salt
2 eggs
¾ cup firmly packed light brown sugar
½ cup safflower or other high-quality vegetable oil
2 tablespoons freshly squeezed orange juice
1½ teaspoons minced or grated orange zest
1 teaspoon vanilla extract
1¼ cups unbleached all-purpose flour
1 teaspoon baking powder
½ teaspoon baking soda
1 teaspoon freshly grated nutmeg
½ teaspoon ground cinnamon
½ cup golden raisins
1 tablespoon granulated sugar mixed with 1 teaspoon freshly grated nutmeg

Summer Squash Pie

Reminiscent of apple pie, here's a sweet way to use up some of late summer's abundant squash. Peeled and sliced chayote (page 40), shown here, also works very well; wear rubber gloves when peeling to protect your skin from the strong enzymes present in the squash. Blanch the slices in boiling water for about 5 minutes instead of using the salt method to remove excess moisture.

Prepare the pastry dough, divide into 2 equal-sized balls, wrap, and chill for 30 minutes.

Place 1 ball of the chilled dough on a lightly floured surface or between 2 sheets of waxed paper. Flatten into a disk and, with a rolling pin, quickly roll with light strokes from the center almost to the edge, rotating the disk slowly so that the strokes radiate outward in a sunburst pattern. Continue to roll in this manner until you form a disk about 13 inches in diameter. Loosely wrap the dough around the rolling pin and transfer it to a 9-inch pie pan. Working from the center outwards, gently press the dough onto the bottom and sides of the pan. Trim edge of crust with a sharp knife, leaving about a ½-inch overhang all around.

In a large bowl, toss the squash slices with the sugar, flour, cinnamon, salt, lemon juice and zest, and nutmeg to taste. Transfer to the pastry-lined pie pan, mounding slightly in the center. Dot with butter.

Preheat an oven to 425° F.

Roll out the remaining ball of dough in the same manner as for the bottom crust. Cut into 1-inch-wide strips with a fluted pastry cutter or sharp knife held against a ruler or other straight edge. Weave the strips in a lattice pattern over the pie filling, pressing firmly at the edges to secure the strips to the pastry shell. Fold the edges of the crust inward and crimp the dough all around with your fingertips to form a decorative pattern. Brush the lattice top with egg white and sprinkle with sugar. Bake for 25 minutes, then reduce the heat to 350° F. and continue baking until golden brown, about 30 minutes longer.

Makes 1 9-inch double-crust pie; serves 6.

Favorite pastry dough recipe for
1 9-inch double-crust pie

SQUASH FILLING
4 cups sliced summer squash
   (about 1⅓ pounds, peeled and
   seeded if large), salted, drained,
   and dried as directed on page 12
1¼ cups granulated sugar
2 tablespoons unbleached all-purpose
   flour
1½ teaspoons ground cinnamon
⅛ teaspoon salt
2 tablespoons freshly squeezed
   lemon juice
1 tablespoon minced lemon zest
Freshly grated nutmeg
2 tablespoons unsalted butter,
   cut into small pieces

1 egg white, beaten
Granulated sugar

Summer Squash Cake with Peanut Frosting

SUMMER SQUASH CAKE
2 cups unbleached all-purpose flour
1 tablespoon ground cinnamon
2 teaspoons baking soda
1 teaspoon salt
1½ cups safflower or other
     high-quality vegetable oil
2 cups granulated sugar
4 eggs
3 cups (about 1 pound) grated
     or finely chopped summer squash
1½ cups butterscotch chips (optional)

PEANUT FROSTING
8 ounces cream cheese, softened
½ cup peanut butter, softened
4 tablespoons (½ stick) unsalted
     butter, softened
2 cups sifted powdered sugar
1 teaspoon bourbon or vanilla extract
2 cups finely chopped unsalted
     roasted peanuts

Happy eaters will find it hard to believe that squash is responsible for this moist cake.

Preheat an oven to 350° F. Grease and lightly flour 2 9-inch round cake pans.

To make the cake, sift the flour, cinnamon, baking soda, and salt together in a bowl; reserve.

In a separate bowl, combine the oil and sugar and beat well. Add the eggs and beat well. Fold the dry ingredients into the wet mixture until well blended. Stir in the squash and butterscotch chips, if using. Spoon into the prepared pans and bake until the tops spring back when touched with a fingertip, about 35 to 45 minutes. Remove from the oven and cool on a wire rack for about 5 minutes. Turn out onto the wire rack to cool completely.

To make the frosting, combine the cream cheese, peanut butter, and butter in a bowl and beat with an electric mixer until smooth. Add the powdered sugar and bourbon or vanilla and beat until smooth.

Place a cooled cake layer, bottom side up, on a serving plate. Spread with some of the frosting and center second layer, bottom side down, on top. Cover the top and sides of the cake with remaining frosting, then press the chopped peanuts evenly onto the sides of the cake.

Makes 1 9-inch two-layer cake; serves 12.

WINTER SQUASH

"If it were not for pumpkins, we'd be undone soon," penned an American colonist in a 1693 diary, indicating the vital importance of these native squash to the earliest settlers. Fortunately for modern cooks, we're no longer limited to pumpkins, but have access to the fruits or seeds of numerous hard-shelled squash cultivars that are the products of modern plant hybridization.

Some of my favorite winter squash do not store or ship as well as 'Acorn,' 'Butternut,' 'Banana,' and other supermarket mainstays. 'Buttercup,' 'Delicata,' and 'Sweet Dumpling' are definitely worth growing in your garden or searching out in farmers' markets, specialty produce stores, and roadside growers' stands. With the exception of 'Vegetable Spaghetti' and Chinese winter melon, winter squash may be used interchangeably in most of the recipes that follow.

WINTER SQUASH NUTRITION

A University of California at Davis study of 25 vegetable crops found winter squash to be among the most nutritious, rivaling cabbage, carrots, potatoes, and spinach. Winter squash are tasty sources of complex carbohydrates and fiber and provide potassium, niacin, and iron. The orange flesh is very high in beta carotene, the source of vitamin A; the deeper the color, the higher the beta carotene content. Although the flesh is a source of incomplete protein, the missing essential fatty acids are found in the edible seeds, which are 38 to 50 percent unsaturated fat and 30 to 40 percent protein.

Like their summer relatives, winter squash are low in sodium and in calories, ranging from 29 to 43 calories per 4-ounce serving.

THE NATIVES

ACORN (*Cucurbita Pepo* 'Acorn'). Also known as Danish squash, this small squash is named for its shape. Look for skin in shades of dark green, orange, or cream. Some of the best varieties are 'Table King,' 'Des Moines,' and 'Queen Anne.'

BANANA (*C. maxima* 'Banana'). A tasty cylindrical squash cultivar, usually sold in chunks, with gray skin that turns creamy pink when stored; very high water content.

BUTTERCUP (*C. maxima* 'Buttercup'). This drum-shaped, broadly ribbed squash gets many connoisseurs' vote as the most flavorful winter squash. Skin is dark green with gray spots and a lighter green topknot at the blossom end; flesh is golden. 'Sweet Mama' is an excellent cultivar.

BUTTERNUT (*C. moschata* 'Butternut'). Smooth, tan long-necked squash with a relatively small seed cavity and excellent flavor and texture; the most widely grown winter squash.

DELICATA (*C. Pepo* 'Delicata'). Shaped like a large cucumber, this sweet-tasting squash is patterned with green, cream, yellow, and orange stripes.

GOLDEN NUGGET (*C. maxima* 'Golden Nugget'). A small, sweet cultivar that mimics pumpkin in shape and color.

HUBBARD (*C. maxima* 'Hubbard'). An old-favorite large squash shaped like a spinning top, in colors ranging from pale green to golden to blue gray; bumpy skinned and with dull orange, fairly dry flesh.

PUMPKIN (*C. maxima*, *C. moschata*, and *C. Pepo*). If you want big pumpkins for prizes or just for show, grow or purchase 'Big Max,' 'Atlantic Giant,' or one of the other varieties that can reach up to 600 pounds. At the other end of the scale are the miniature pumpkins such as 'Jack Be Little' that are best used for decorations, even though they are edible. For Halloween carving, there's 'Cinderella,' 'Funny Face,' 'Jack-O'-Lantern,' and others. But for cooking, choose the more flavorful cultivars that taste as good as they sound—'Small Sugar,' 'New England Pie,' 'Triple Treat.'

SPAGHETTI (*C. Pepo* 'Vegetable Spaghetti'). An oval-shaped yellow squash with flesh that forms long noodlelike strands when cooked.

SWEET DUMPLING (*C. Pepo* 'Sweet Dumpling'). Small, vertically striped squash with deep ridges, a flattened top, and exceptionally sweet flesh.

TURK'S TURBAN (*C. maxima* 'Turbaniformis'). As the name suggests, this vividly colored squash is capped with a turbanlike apex. Often used decoratively although quite edible, it is not as tasty as some of the other winter varieties.

THE ASIANS

CHINESE WINTER MELON (*Benincasa hispida*). Sold in Cantonese markets as *dung gwa*, I've included this large tropical Asian native of the cucumber family with the winter squash because its hard skin makes it ideal for long storage. The blue-gray-green skin is covered with a splotchy white film, giving the winter melon the look of a watermelon dusted with powdery snow. Its common name is further enhanced by a seed cavity resembling an ice and snow cavern, and by soft, snowy white, delicate-tasting flesh.

JAPANESE PUMPKIN (*C. moschata*). Also known by its Japanese name *kabocha* or its Cantonese name *nam gwa*, the green skin of this delicious squash is mottled with gray or brown; 'Red Kuri' is a brilliant orange-skinned variety. Although thought of as an Asian vegetable, the Japanese pumpkin is actually a Western hemisphere native that made its way to Malaysia, then to China, and finally to Japan, where it was improved over the last few centuries before returning to its American homeland. Several varieties are sold here in Japanese markets and specialty produce shops.

Preparing Winter Squash
for Cooking

CHOOSING WINTER SQUASH

Winter squash should feel firm and heavy for their size. Look for hard skin free of soft spots, cracks, or discolored areas, although slight variation in skin pigmentation is acceptable.

When buying by the piece, avoid those with bruises, blemishes, uneven coloring, or watery-looking flesh.

In general, a 1½-pound squash yields about 3½ cups diced, chopped, or grated squash, or enough to serve 4 people.

Most recipes call for squash to be cut in half or in pieces. Position the squash on a large cutting surface so that the stem end is facing away from you. Place the blade of a heavy, sharp chef's knife or cleaver horizontally along the length of the squash. With a hammer or wooden mallet, repeatedly hit the back of the blade at the point where it joins the handle to drive it into the squash until the squash breaks in half. Use the same technique to cut smaller pieces from each half, if necessary.

With a metal spoon, scoop out the seeds and any interior stringy portions. Frugal cooks can add the stringy fibers to flavor vegetable stock that will be strained before using. All squash seeds are edible, although few varieties bear hull-less seeds that do not need shelling before eating. To use the seeds, wash to separate them from the stringy matter, then blot dry with paper toweling. To toast as a snack, spread the seeds in a single layer on a baking sheet and sprinkle with seasoned salt, garlic pepper, ground cayenne pepper, chili powder, or other seasonings as desired. Place in a 300° F. oven until crisp and toasted, about 20 to 25 minutes. Cool and store in a container with a tight-fitting cover.

Peel the squash with a swivel-blade vegetable peeler or small, sharp paring knife. Most people find it simpler to peel the squash after it has been cut into halves or pieces. Once peeled, the squash can be easily cut into smaller pieces as desired.

Cooking Winter Squash

These basic techniques are intended to serve as a guide for you to create your own household's favorite dishes.

BAKING. Cut squash in half or in pieces and scoop out seeds as directed on page 56; do not peel. If you plan to serve the squash half, cut off a small slice from the bottom so it will stand upright. Brush the surface of the flesh with melted butter and season to taste with salt. Arrange, cut side down, in a baking dish, add water to a depth of about ¼ inch, and bake in a preheated 400° F. oven until tender when pierced with a fork or skewer, about 45 minutes to 1 hour.

If you plan to serve the squash in its shell, turn upright after 30 minutes and brush with more melted butter, sprinkle with brown sugar or drizzle with maple syrup or honey to taste, and dust with spices such as cinnamon or nutmeg and salt and pepper to taste. Continue cooking, basting occasionally with more melted butter, until tender. If you intend to purée the cooked squash, remove it from the oven when tender and let stand until cool enough to handle. Peel off and discard the skin or scoop the flesh from the skin. Purée the flesh, or use as directed in recipes.

For baked stuffed halves, fill and cook as directed on page 76.

To bake whole small winter squash, pierce the shell in several places with a long-tined fork or a metal skewer to allow steam to escape during baking. Place in a baking dish, add water to a depth of ¼ inch, and bake in a preheated 400° F. oven until the skin begins to shrivel and gives when pressed with your fingertips, about 30 to 40 minutes. Remove from the oven. Wearing oven mitts, position the squash on a cutting surface with the stem end away from you and slice in half lengthwise. Remove seeds and any stringy portions. Return squash to the baking dish, cut side up, brush the flesh with melted butter, and bake until tender when pierced with a fork.

To bake pumpkins, 'Buttercup,' and other whole round squash to serve as edible containers, follow recipe directions on page 75, eliminating the filling.

STORING WINTER SQUASH

Most winter squash that are free of bruises can be stored in a cool, dry, dark place such as an attic or a garage for up to 6 months. Ideal temperature is between 45° and 50° F. Some of the smaller types like 'Acorn' and 'Delicata' keep for only about half as long. To prevent deterioration, do not refrigerate or store in a damp place.

Squash purchased by the piece should be tightly wrapped and refrigerated for no more than 4 days.

Winter squash cooked by any of the accompanying basic methods can be tightly covered and refrigerated for up to a week. Puréed or mashed cooked squash, plain or seasoned, can be successfully frozen for up to 6 months.

PURÉEING WINTER SQUASH

Bake (page 57) or steam (page 59) the squash until very tender. When cool enough to handle, scrape the flesh from the shell with a spoon into a food processor or blender. Or transfer peeled cooked squash pieces to a food processor or blender. Purée until smooth.

Use puréed squash as directed in recipes or season to taste with melted butter, salt, a sweetener, and spices such as cinnamon, cloves, or ginger. To serve, reheat in a saucepan over medium-low heat or in a microwave oven.

Plain canned pumpkin purée can be substituted in most recipes when fresh winter squash is unavailable.

As a general rule, 1 pound of raw winter squash yields 1½ to 2 cups of purée.

BOILING OR SIMMERING. Place whole squash or large pieces (prepared as directed on page 56) in a saucepan or stockpot. Add water to cover by 1 inch. Place over high heat and boil until tender when pierced with a fork or skewer; cooking time will vary according to size and type of squash. Remove from the water and let stand until cool enough to handle. Cut whole squash in half lengthwise and remove seeds and stringy portions. Peel off and discard skin or scoop flesh from the halves or pieces. Purée the flesh, or use as directed in recipes.

Alternatively, peel and seed the squash, cut into small cubes or slices, and add to soups or stews. Simmer until tender, about 15 minutes.

MICROWAVING. Prepare squash pieces as directed on page 56. Cut peeled and cleaned squash into pieces about 2 inches thick. Arrange in a single layer in a glass dish, season to taste or as directed in recipes, cover with plastic wrap or a microwave lid, and cook on high, turning once, until tender, about 8 to 10 minutes. Serve, purée, or use as directed in recipes.

To cook small squash such as 'Acorn' or 'Sweet Dumpling,' cut in half and scoop out seeds and stringy portions. Place squash in a glass plate, season to taste, cover with a microwave lid or plastic wrap, and cook on high, turning once or twice, until tender, about 12 to 15 minutes. Serve, purée the flesh, or use as directed in recipes.

SAUTÉING. Prepare squash halves or pieces as directed on page 56. Cut peeled and cleaned squash into slices about 3 to 4 inches long and about ¼ inch thick, or grate the squash. Heat about 2 tablespoons butter or high-quality vegetable oil per cup of squash in a sauté pan or skillet, add the squash, and cook, turning the slices frequently, until tender when pierced with a fork or wooden skewer and browned on both sides, about 10 to 15 minutes. Proceed in the same way for grated squash, continuously moving it about the pan so that it does not burn and sautéing until tender, about 6 to 8 minutes. Season to taste.

STEAMING. Prepare squash halves or pieces as directed on page 56. Place squash on a rack set over boiling water. Cover tightly and steam until the squash is tender when pierced with a fork or skewer, about 20 to 30 minutes. Add boiling water to the pan as necessary to maintain level.

A FEW EXTRA IDEAS

Peel and thinly slice small winter squash and serve raw as part of a crudités presentation, or add to mixed green or vegetable salads. Or shred and use in place of cabbage in slaw.

Simmer chunks of peeled winter squash in stews or pot roasts, remove them with a slotted spoon when tender, then mash the squash and stir it back into the pot to thicken the gravy.

Add grated winter squash to your favorite bread stuffing for fowl.

Include peeled winter squash slices with more traditional vegetables when batter frying foods for Japanese *tempura* or Italian *fritto misto*.

For a real treat, fill fresh pasta squares or rounds with the purée to make ravioli or tortellini. Simmer in flavorful stock and serve with a simple cream sauce and a grating of nutmeg.

Add about 1 cup puréed cooked winter squash to your basic cornbread recipe; increase cooking time to account for extra moisture.

For a change in flavor, experiment with cooked winter squash other than pumpkin in your favorite Thanksgiving pie recipe.

Fried Winter Squash Chips

1-pound piece winter squash
Safflower or other high-quality
    vegetable oil for deep frying
Salt

Vary these snacks by sprinkling the drained chips with a favorite seasoning such as ground cayenne pepper, a blend of sweet winter spices, garlic or other flavored salt, or curry powder. I often use the long neck end of 'Butternut' or 'Tahitian' because the elongated shape is easy to slice.

Peel the squash and slice paper thin. Place in a bowl, cover with ice water, and let stand for about 1 hour. Drain and blot completely dry with paper toweling.

Pour oil into a deep fryer or saucepan to a depth of 3 inches. Set over high heat and heat to 375° F., or until a small piece of bread dropped into the oil turns golden within seconds. Working in batches, carefully transfer squash slices to the hot oil with a frying basket or slotted spoon; do not crowd the slices. Cook, stirring frequently, until the chips are lightly browned and crisp, about 10 minutes. Drain on paper toweling and sprinkle with salt to taste. Serve warm or at room temperature.

Serves 6.

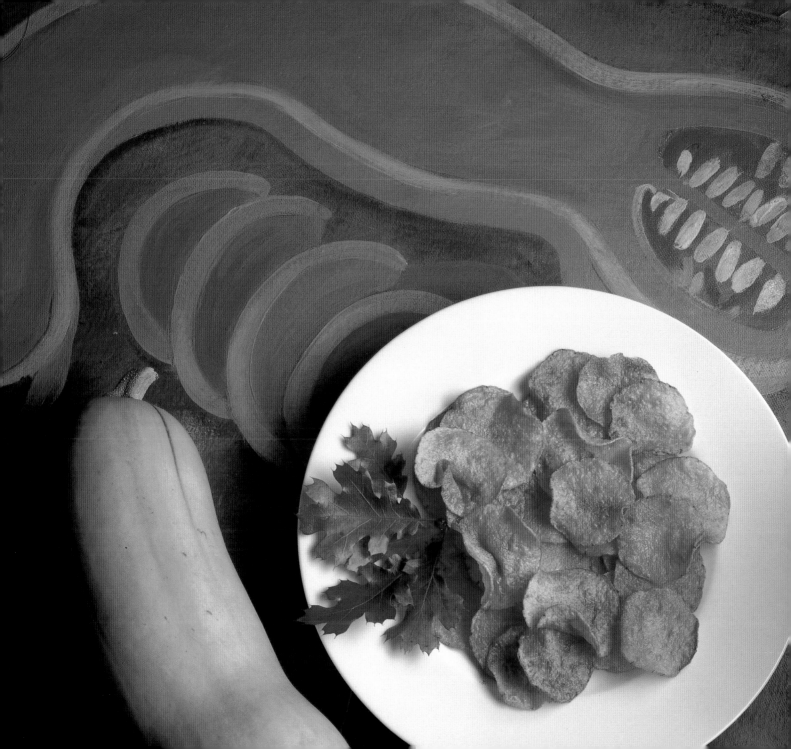

Creamy Winter Squash Soup

Although I usually prepare this soup with pumpkin, other winter squash such as 'Buttercup,' 'Butternut,' or 'Hubbard' can be used with excellent results.

To prepare an edible serving bowl, cut off and reserve the top of a large whole squash of the same type used to prepare the soup. With a spoon, scoop out the seeds and stringy portions, replace the top, and wrap the stem with foil to prevent it from burning. Place in a shallow pan containing about ½ inch of water and bake in a preheated 350° F. oven until the pumpkin is tender but still holds its shape, about 1 hour.

In a large, heavy saucepan, melt the butter over medium-high heat. Add the leek and shallot and sauté until very tender and golden, about 8 minutes. Add the pumpkin or other squash and chicken stock or broth. Bring to a boil, cover, reduce heat to low, and simmer until the squash is tender, about 30 minutes. (If using pumpkin or other squash purée, simmer about 15 minutes.)

Working in batches, transfer to a food processor or blender and purée. Place in a clean saucepan, add the cream or half and half, orange juice, ginger, and salt and pepper to taste. Place over medium heat, stirring frequently, until hot; do not boil. Carefully pour into baked pumpkin shell, if desired (see recipe introduction). Ladle into preheated bowls, add a dollop of crème fraîche or sour cream, and garnish with toasted hazelnuts and orange zest.

Serves 6.

NOTE: To toast hazelnuts, place in a shallow pan in a 350° F. oven, stirring frequently, until the nuts are golden under their skins. Transfer to a plate to cool. Rub nuts between fingertips to remove skins.

4 tablespoons unsalted butter
1 cup chopped leek, white part only
½ cup chopped shallot
1½ pounds pumpkin or other winter squash, peeled, cleaned, and cut into ½-inch chunks, or 3 cups puréed cooked pumpkin or other winter squash (page 58), from about 1½ pounds raw squash
1 quart homemade chicken stock or canned chicken broth
1 cup heavy (whipping) cream, light cream, or half and half
1 cup freshly squeezed orange juice
½ teaspoon ground ginger
Salt
Freshly ground white pepper
Crème fraîche or sour cream
Chopped toasted hazelnuts for garnish (see note)
Minced orange zest for garnish

Chinese Winter Melon Pond Soup

1 10- to 12-pound winter melon
  (page 55)
2½ quarts homemade chicken stock
  or canned chicken broth
1 whole chicken breast, boned,
  skinned, and cut into bite-sized
  pieces
10 ounces boneless pork, cut into
  bite-sized pieces
1 tablespoon peeled and minced
  fresh ginger root
1 tablespoon minced tangerine
  or orange zest
½ cup dried lotus seeds, soaked
  in hot water for 30 minutes,
  then drained (optional)
½ cup peeled and thinly sliced
  fresh lotus root (optional)
½ cup sliced canned bamboo shoot
½ cup sliced fresh *shiitake*
  mushrooms, or 6 dried Asian
  black mushrooms, soaked in
  warm water for 30 minutes,
  then drained, stems discarded,
  and sliced
¼ cup thinly sliced green onion,
  including some of the green tops
⅓ cup diced flavorful baked ham
½ cup drained canned gingko nuts
  (optional)
1 tablespoon soy sauce, or to taste
Salt

When serving this spectacular soup, be sure to scoop out some of the soft white pulp from the edible container. A much simpler version can be made by cooking ½ pound winter melon, peeled and cut into chunks, in the stock and serving the soup in bowls.

To prepare the winter melon as a serving container, wash the exterior, scrubbing the skin well with a stiff brush to remove the waxy coating. Slice off a thin portion from the bottom of the squash if needed to make it stand upright. Cut off the top as you would if carving a jack-o'-lantern, reserving this piece for a lid. Using a large spoon, scoop out seeds and stringy portions.

If you wish to carve a design on the outside of the winter melon, draw a pattern on a sheet of paper large enough to wrap around the exterior. Trace the pattern onto the melon with a ball-point pen, using just enough pressure to leave an indention in the skin. With a small sharp knife, pare away the green skin from the background of the design.

Preheat an oven to 350° F.

Position the winter melon in a shallow baking pan, pour in hot water to a depth of 2 inches, and bake until the flesh is soft to the touch when pressed, about 1½ to 2 hours.

To make the soup, combine the chicken stock or broth, chicken meat, pork, ginger, tangerine or orange zest, and lotus seeds and root, if using, in a saucepan over medium heat. Bring to a simmer, cover, and simmer for 25 minutes. Stir in the bamboo shoot, mushrooms, green onion, ham, and gingko nuts, if using, and simmer until the meats are cooked and other ingredients are heated through, about 10 minutes longer. Season with the soy sauce and salt to taste. Transfer the soup to the cooked winter melon bowl and deliver to the table immediately. Ladle into small bowls to serve, scooping some of the cooked flesh into each bowl.

Serves 8 to 10.

Glazed Winter Squash with Pine Nuts

Both squash and pine nuts were major foods of many native American tribes. I've teamed them in this comforting winter dish that's especially appropriate for the Thanksgiving feast.

Place the pine nuts in a small dry skillet over medium heat and cook, stirring frequently, until lightly toasted, about 5 minutes. Pour onto a plate to cool. Reserve.

Melt 2 tablespoons of the butter in a sauté pan or skillet over medium heat. Add the onion and cook, stirring often, until very soft and golden, about 10 minutes. Stir in the garlic and sauté 1 minute longer. Remove from the heat and reserve.

Preheat an oven to 425° F.

Combine the squash, heavy cream, light cream or half and half, thyme, coriander, and mace in a heavy-bottomed saucepan. Bring to a boil over medium-high heat. Reduce the heat to low and simmer, uncovered, until the squash is tender and has absorbed most of the liquid, about 15 minutes. Season to taste with salt and pepper.

Toss squash mixture with the reserved onion and transfer to a lightly greased 8-by-12-inch baking dish. Sprinkle with the cheese and dot with the remaining 4 tablespoons butter. Bake for 10 minutes, then sprinkle with the toasted pine nuts. Continue baking until the top is lightly browned, about 5 minutes longer. Serve immediately.

Serves 10 to 12.

3/4 cup pine nuts
6 tablespoons unsalted butter
1½ cups chopped yellow onion
2 teaspoons minced or pressed garlic
4 pounds 'Buttercup,' 'Butternut,' 'Sweet Mama,' or other winter squash, peeled, cleaned, and cut into slices ⅜ inch thick
2 cups heavy (whipping) cream
2 cups light cream or half and half
1 teaspoon minced fresh thyme, or ¼ teaspoon crumbled dried thyme
½ teaspoon ground coriander
¼ teaspoon ground mace
Salt
Freshly ground black pepper
½ cup freshly grated dry Monterey Jack or Parmesan cheese

Spaghetti Squash with Cheese

Strands of cooked spaghetti squash can be tossed with plain butter or with butter flavored with herbs, fruit, or nuts. They can also be topped with a favorite pasta sauce such as marinara, mushroom, clam, pesto, or creamy Alfredo.

After mixing the squash strands with the selected sauce, I like to heap it back into the shell halves for serving. Unsauced strands can be stored in the refrigerator and reheated by steaming or microwaving briefly.

To bake the squash, preheat an oven to 325° F.

With a fork, pierce the squash in several places with a long-tined fork or metal skewer to prevent the shell from bursting during cooking. Place the squash in a baking pan. Bake until the shell gives a bit when pressed, or until the flesh is easily pierced with a fork, about 1½ to 2 hours. Alternatively, immerse the squash in a large pot of boiling water and cook until it is easily pierced, about 45 minutes.

Melt the butter in a skillet or saucepan over medium-low heat. Add the garlic and cook until tender but not browned, about 5 minutes. If desired, strain and discard the garlic. Keep the butter warm.

When cool enough to handle, cut the squash in half lengthwise and scoop out seeds and stringy portions. Using a fork, pull pulp from the shell in long strands and put them in a heated bowl. Add the garlic butter, grated cheese, and salt and pepper to taste and toss to blend well. Garnish with minced basil or parsley, if desired, and serve immediately. Pass additional cheese at the table.

Serves 6.

1 4- to 5-pound spaghetti squash
¼ pound (1 stick) unsalted butter
1 tablespoon minced or pressed garlic, or to taste
1 cup freshly grated Parmesan cheese, preferably Parmigiano-Reggiano
Salt
Freshly ground white pepper
Minced fresh basil or parsley, preferably flat-leaf type, for garnish (optional)
Additional Parmesan cheese for passing

Winter Squash Risotto

1½-pound piece winter squash
1½ cups short-grain white rice,
    preferably *arborio* or pearl
About 6 cups homemade vegetable
    or chicken stock or canned
    chicken broth
¼ pound (1 stick) unsalted butter
½ cup minced shallot or yellow onion
1 teaspoon minced or pressed garlic
½ cup dry white wine
½ cup freshly grated Parmesan cheese,
    preferably Parmigiano-Reggiano
Salt
Freshly ground black pepper
Chopped fresh dill (optional)
Additional Parmesan cheese
    for passing

Italy's famous rice dish is exceptionally flavorful when made with 'Buttercup,' 'Butternut,' or one of the pumpkin varieties.

Peel and clean the squash and cut the pulp into ½-inch cubes. Reserve.

Vigorously wash the rice under running cold water, drain, and reserve.

In a saucepan, bring the stock or broth to a boil over high heat, then reduce the heat to low and keep the broth at a simmer during the rest of the cooking.

Heat 7 tablespoons of the butter in a heavy, deep sauté pan or skillet over medium-high heat. Add the shallot or onion and sauté until lightly golden, about 5 minutes. Add the squash and 1 cup of the chicken stock and cook about 5 minutes. Stir in the garlic and drained rice and sauté until all the grains of the rice are well coated, about 2 minutes. Stir in the white wine and cook, stirring, until the wine has evaporated, about 3 minutes. Add ½ cup of the simmering stock. Keep the liquid and rice at a simmer and gently stir almost continuously, scraping the bottom and sides of the pan, until the liquid has been absorbed. Adjust the heat if the liquid is evaporating too quickly.

Add hot stock ½ cup at a time each time the rice becomes dry, continuing to stir. As the risotto approaches completion, add the liquid only ¼ cup at a time. You may not need all the stock before the rice is done, or you may need more liquid, in which case add hot water. Cook until the rice is tender but firm to the bite, about 25 minutes total. When properly cooked, the rice should be creamy but not soupy.

A couple of minutes before you think the rice will be done, stir in the cheese and the remaining 1 tablespoon butter. Add salt and pepper to taste. Sprinkle with dill, if using, and serve immediately. Pass additional Parmesan at the table.

Serves 4 to 6 as a first course or side dish.

Sautéed Pumpkin
with Green Pumpkin Seed Sauce

PUMPKIN SEED SAUCE
1 cup plus 2 tablespoons untoasted
   hulled green pumpkin seeds
   (*pepitas*)
3 or 4 fresh hot red or green chili
   peppers, or to taste, stemmed,
   seeded, if desired, and coarsely
   chopped
1 cup coarsely chopped fresh parsley,
   preferably flat-leaf type
½ cup coarsely chopped fresh cilantro
   (coriander)
½ cup chopped yellow onion
2 teaspoons minced or pressed garlic
¼ teaspoon ground cumin
½ teaspoon ground cinnamon
⅛ teaspoon ground cloves
2 tablespoons safflower or olive oil
3 cups homemade chicken stock
   or canned chicken broth
Salt
Freshly ground black pepper

SAUTÉED PUMPKIN
About 2 tablespoons unsalted butter
About 2 tablespoons safflower or
   other high-quality vegetable oil
1-pound piece pumpkin, peeled,
   cleaned, and cut into uniform
   ½-inch-thick slices
Salt
Freshly ground black pepper
Chopped fresh cilantro (coriander)
   for garnish

In Mexico, pumpkin seed sauce (*salsa verde de semillas de calabaza*) is poured over poached chicken or fish, which you may choose to use instead of the sautéed pumpkin slices. Look for untoasted hulled green seeds, or *pepitas*, in natural-foods stores or Spanish or Latin American groceries.

To make the sauce, place the pumpkin seeds in a dry skillet over medium-low heat, and cook, stirring constantly, until they pop and are lightly toasted, about 5 minutes. Pour onto a plate to cool.

In a food processor or blender, combine 1 cup of the cooled pumpkin seeds, chili peppers, parsley, cilantro, onion, garlic, cumin, cinnamon, cloves, oil, and ½ cup of the chicken stock or broth. Blend as smoothly as possible. Transfer to a saucepan. Add the remaining 2½ cups chicken stock and bring to a boil over medium-high heat. Season to taste with salt and pepper, reduce the heat to low, partially cover, and simmer until slightly thickened, about 30 minutes. Taste and adjust seasonings.

To sauté the pumpkin slices, heat 2 tablespoons each butter and oil in a sauté pan or skillet over medium-high heat. Add the pumpkin slices and cook, turning occasionally, until the pumpkin slices are browned and tender but still hold their shape, about 15 minutes total cooking time; add a little additional butter and/or oil if pumpkin begins to stick. Drain briefly on paper toweling and season to taste with salt and pepper.

To serve, arrange the pumpkin slices on individual plates, spoon some of the sauce over or alongside the slices, and garnish with chopped cilantro and the remaining 2 tablespoons pumpkin seeds.

Serves 4.

Cheese-Stuffed Whole Winter Squash

Traditionally made with pumpkin, this classic dish adapts to 'Buttercup,' 'Golden Delicious,' *kabocha* (Japanese pumpkin), and other globular varieties. Mildly flavored Turk's turban, usually prized for autumn decor rather than as a culinary treat, is quite a showy container. Small squash such as 'Acorn,' 'Sweet Dumpling,' or even tiny miniature pumpkins could be transformed into individual serving bowls.

Cut off and reserve the top of the squash to use as a lid. With a large spoon, scoop out the seeds and stringy portions. Reserve.

Preheat an oven to 400° F.

Heat the butter in a sauté pan or skillet over medium heat. Add the onion and cook until very soft and golden, about 10 minutes. Stir in the garlic and cook 1 minute longer. Add the bread crumbs and stir to coat thoroughly with butter. Remove from the heat and combine with the cheese, heavy cream, 1 cup of the light cream or half and half, and salt, pepper, and nutmeg to taste.

Place the squash in a shallow baking pan. Fill the squash to within ½ inch of the rim with the cheese mixture, adding more half and half if necessary to reach this level. Cover with the reserved lid and wrap the stem with foil to prevent it from burning. Bake until the cheese mixture is bubbly and the shell of the squash is soft to the touch on the outside, about 1 hour.

Transport the squash to the table for serving and remove the lid. With a long-handled spoon, scoop out some of the cooked pulp along with the melted cheese stuffing for each serving.

Serves 6 to 8.

1 4- to 5-pound whole winter squash
¼ pound (1 stick) unsalted butter
1 cup finely chopped yellow onion
1 teaspoon minced or pressed garlic
1¾ cups unseasoned fine dry bread crumbs, preferably from French bread
¾ cup freshly shredded Swiss cheese, preferably Emmentaler
1 cup heavy (whipping) cream
About 1½ cups light cream or half and half
Salt
Freshly ground black pepper
Freshly grated nutmeg

Cranberry-Stuffed Winter Squash

2 small winter squash
1 tablespoon unsalted butter, melted
Salt
2 tablespoons unsalted butter
½ cup minced shallot or finely
    chopped yellow onion
1 teaspoon minced or pressed garlic
2 cups coarsely chopped unpeeled
    tart apple (3 or 4 apples)
½ cup coarsely chopped fresh
    cranberries
½ teaspoon ground cinnamon
¼ teaspoon freshly grated nutmeg
2 cups unseasoned fine dry bread
    crumbs, preferably from whole-
    wheat or pumpernickel bread
1 cup (about 3 ounces) freshly grated
    Cheddar, Monterey Jack, or
    freshly shredded Swiss cheese,
    preferably Emmentaler
¼ pound sliced smoked bacon

'Acorn' is probably the easiest variety to use for this dish, although 'Delicata,' 'Sweet Dumpling,' and small specimens of other winter squash will also work.

Preheat an oven to 400° F.

Cut the squash in half lengthwise and scoop out seeds and stringy portions as directed on page 56. Brush the cut sides of the squash halves with the melted butter and season to taste with salt. Arrange, cut side down, on a lightly greased baking sheet. Pour in hot water to a depth of ½ inch and bake until barely tender when pierced with a wooden skewer, about 35 to 45 minutes.

Melt 2 tablespoons butter in a sauté pan or skillet over medium-high heat. Add the shallot or onion and sauté until almost soft, about 4 minutes. Stir in the garlic, apple, and cranberries and sauté until the apples are soft, about 4 minutes longer. Stir in the cinnamon and nutmeg.

In a bowl, combine the apple mixture, bread crumbs, and cheese. Mound in the cavities of the baked squash halves and arrange in a baking dish. Bake until the squash is tender, the filling is heated through, and the cheese melts, about 20 minutes.

Meanwhile, fry the bacon in a skillet until crisp. Drain briefly on paper toweling, then crumble.

Remove the squash from the oven, sprinkle with the crumbled bacon, and serve hot.

Serves 4 as a side dish, or 2 as a main course.

Golden Yeast Rolls

Instead of fashioning the dough into predictable rounds, treat it in one of the following ways: cut the dough into strips about 9 inches long by 2 inches wide and loosely tie each into a knot; cut these same long strips in half lengthwise and braid them together; roll the dough into small balls and place 3 together in each well of a muffin tin to bake into cloverleaf shapes; or cut dough into pie-wedge shapes, roll up from the broad end, and turn corners to form crescents.

In a small bowl, dissolve the sugar in the warm water. Sprinkle the yeast over the water and stir gently until it dissolves. Let stand in a warm spot until a thin layer of foam covers the surface, about 5 minutes, indicating that the yeast is effective.

In a mixing bowl, combine the foamy yeast, warm milk, melted butter, and salt; beat to blend thoroughly. Stir in 1 cup of the flour. Beat in the squash purée, then stir in just as much of the remaining flour as needed to form a soft dough that can be easily handled. Turn out onto a lightly floured surface and knead until the dough is no longer sticky, about 5 minutes, adding more flour, a little at a time, if necessary. Form into a ball and place in a buttered bowl, turning dough to coat all sides with butter. Cover the bowl tightly with plastic wrap and set in a warm place until the dough is doubled in size, about 1 hour.

On a lightly floured surface, roll out the dough into a disk about ½ inch thick. Cut into rounds that are 3 to 4 inches in diameter. Place rounds about ½ inch apart on a parchment-lined or lightly greased baking sheet. Cover rolls loosely with plastic wrap or a cloth kitchen towel and let them stand in a warm place until they rise to about 1½ times their size, about 30 minutes.

Preheat the oven to 400° F.

Brush the tops of the rolls with melted butter and sprinkle with seeds, if desired. Bake until lightly golden, about 20 minutes. Transfer from the baking sheet at once to a wire rack to cool briefly. Serve hot.

Makes about 14 3-inch round rolls.

2 tablespoons granulated sugar
¼ cup warm water, about 110° F.
1 envelope (¼ ounce or 1 tablespoon) active dry yeast
1 cup warm milk, about 110° F.
3 tablespoons unsalted butter, melted
1 teaspoon salt
About 4 cups sifted unbleached all-purpose flour
1 cup puréed cooked winter squash (page 58), from about ½ pound peeled and cleaned raw squash
Melted unsalted butter for brushing tops
Sesame or poppy seeds for sprinkling (optional)

Squash Pancakes

Prepare this breakfast or supper treat with puréed 'Butternut,' 'Hubbard,' or other winter varieties. When you're in a hurry, substitute plain canned pumpkin purée. Serve with melted butter and warmed maple syrup or applesauce.

In a bowl, sift together the flour, baking powder, salt, allspice, and cinnamon. Reserve.

Beat the egg in a separate bowl, add the squash purée, maple syrup or molasses, milk or buttermilk, and melted butter. Blend in the dry ingredients to form a smooth batter.

To make each pancake, spoon a heaping tablespoon of batter onto a lightly greased preheated griddle, flatten with a spoon to about ½-inch thickness, and cook until the bottom side is golden brown, about 3 to 4 minutes. Turn and cook on the other side until golden brown, about 5 minutes longer. Grease griddle as needed to prevent burning. Serve immediately.

Makes about 24 3-inch pancakes; serves 4 to 6.

VARIATIONS: Stir ½ cup chopped walnuts, pecans, or hazelnuts into the batter just before cooking.

Use 1 part whole-wheat or buckwheat flour and 2 parts unbleached all-purpose flour.

1 cup unbleached all-purpose flour
1 teaspoon baking powder
½ teaspoon salt
1 teaspoon ground allspice
½ teaspoon ground cinnamon
1 egg
2 cups puréed cooked winter squash (page 58), from about 1 pound peeled and cleaned raw squash
3 tablespoons maple syrup or molasses, or to taste
3 tablespoons milk or buttermilk
1 tablespoon unsalted butter, melted

Nut-Topped Squash Bread

2 cups unbleached all-purpose flour
1 teaspoon baking soda
½ teaspoon baking powder
½ teaspoon salt
1 teaspoon ground cinnamon
1 teaspoon ground ginger
½ teaspoon freshly grated nutmeg
4 tablespoons unsalted butter,
    softened
1 cup granulated sugar
½ cup honey
2 eggs
1¼ cups puréed cooked winter squash
    (page 58), from about 10 ounces
    peeled and cleaned raw squash
2 tablespoons unsalted butter, melted
½ cup finely chopped pecans
    or walnuts
Powdered sugar for dusting
    (optional)

Equally delicious with afternoon tea, as a breakfast treat, or as a light dessert, this homey loaf makes a welcome gift. Serve with cream cheese or whipped butter sweetened to taste with honey.

Preheat an oven to 350° F.

Sift the flour, baking soda, baking powder, salt, cinnamon, ginger, and nutmeg together in a bowl; reserve.

In a large bowl, cream the butter, sugar, and honey together until light and fluffy. Beat in the eggs. Add the squash purée and beat until smooth. Fold in the reserved dry ingredients. Turn into a greased 9-by-5-inch loaf pan, pour the melted butter over the top, and sprinkle with the chopped nuts.

Bake until golden brown and a wooden skewer inserted in the center comes out clean, about 1 hour. Remove from the oven and let stand 10 minutes before turning out onto a wire rack to cool. Sprinkle with powdered sugar, if desired. Serve warm or at room temperature.

Makes 1 loaf.

Butternut Pie

Although it is perfectly wonderful made with any other full-flavored winter-squash variety, I especially like the richness of 'Butternut' squash for this pie.

To make the crust, butter a 9-inch pie pan. Combine the flour, nuts, sugar, salt, butter, and almond or vanilla extract in a bowl and mix to combine thoroughly. Transfer to the pie pan and press firmly and evenly onto bottom and sides of pan. Cover and refrigerate for 30 minutes.

Preheat an oven to 350° F.

Bake the chilled crust until lightly golden, about 15 to 20 minutes. Set aside to cool.

To make the filling, combine the squash purée, brown sugar, milk, egg yolks, gelatin, cinnamon, ginger, salt, and cloves in a medium-sized saucepan over medium heat. Cook, stirring constantly, until the mixture almost reaches the boiling point. Remove from the heat and cool to room temperature, then refrigerate until the mixture is cold and holds its shape slightly when dropped from a spoon, about 1½ hours.

Beat the egg whites in a small bowl until soft peaks form. Gradually add the granulated sugar and continue beating until the whites are shiny and stiff. Fold the crème fraîche or sour cream and orange zest into the chilled squash mixture, then fold in the egg whites. Spoon into the crust and chill for several hours or as long as overnight.

Just before serving, garnish with crème fraîche or sour cream, fruit slices, and mint leaves, if available.

Makes 1 9-inch pie; serves 6.

NUT CRUST
1 cup unbleached all-purpose flour
½ cup finely chopped pecans or
    walnuts
6 tablespoons granulated sugar
½ teaspoon salt
¼ pound (1 stick) unsalted butter,
    softened
1 teaspoon almond or vanilla extract

BUTTERNUT FILLING
1½ cups puréed cooked 'Butternut'
    or other winter squash (page 58),
    from about 12 ounces peeled
    and cleaned raw squash
¾ cup firmly packed brown sugar
½ cup milk
2 eggs, separated
1 tablespoon (1 envelope) unflavored
    gelatin
1 teaspoon ground cinnamon
¾ teaspoon ground ginger
½ teaspoon salt
¼ teaspoon ground cloves
⅓ cup granulated sugar
½ cup crème fraîche or sour cream
1 teaspoon grated or minced
    orange zest

Additional crème fraîche or sour
    cream, sweetened with granulated
    sugar to taste, for garnish
Fresh kiwi, tangerine, or orange
    slices for garnish
Fresh mint leaves for garnish
    (optional)

Mexican Pumpkin Turnovers

PASTRY
2 cups unbleached all-purpose flour
2 tablespoons granulated sugar
2 teaspoons baking powder
½ teaspoon salt
⅔ cup solid vegetable shortening, chilled
About ¼ cup ice water

FILLING
1 cup puréed cooked pumpkin (page 58), from about ½ pound peeled and cleaned raw pumpkin
¼ cup firmly packed brown sugar
2 teaspoons aniseed
½ teaspoon freshly grated nutmeg
¼ teaspoon salt

1 egg, beaten, or 2 tablespoons unsalted butter, melted
2 tablespoons granulated sugar mixed with 2 teaspoons ground cinnamon

Empanadas con calabaza, spicy sweet pumpkin purée encased in pastry half-moons, are a favorite snack or dessert in Mexico, especially during the Christmas season. Of course, you can use any cooked winter squash in place of pumpkin.

To make the pastry, sift together the flour, sugar, baking powder, and salt into a food processor fitted with a steel blade or a mixing bowl. Add the shortening and cut in with the steel blade or a pastry blender until pieces are about the size of coarse grains. Sprinkle the ice water, a tablespoon at a time, over the dough and mix just until the dough begins to hold together. Form into a ball with your hands, wrap in waxed paper or plastic wrap, and refrigerate for 30 minutes.

To make the filling, combine the pumpkin purée, sugar, aniseed, nutmeg, and salt in a saucepan over medium-high heat. Bring to a boil, then reduce the heat to low and simmer for 10 minutes. Cool to room temperature before using.

Preheat an oven to 400° F.

Roll out the dough on a lightly floured board into a disk about ⅛ inch thick. For *empanadas*, cut the dough into 4- to 5-inch circles; for *empanaditas*, cut into 3-inch circles. Spoon a heaping tablespoon of the filling on one-half of each large circle, or a heaping teaspoon on each small circle. Moisten the edges of the circle with cold water and fold the uncovered side of the circle over the filled side to form a half-moon shape. Press the edges together with the tines of a fork or a rolling fluted pastry wheel. Place the pastries on a lightly greased baking sheet, brush the tops with egg or butter, and bake until golden brown, about 20 minutes. Remove to a wire rack to cool briefly. Sprinkle with sugar-cinnamon mixture while still hot. Serve warm or at room temperature.

Makes about 12 *empanadas*, or 36 *empanaditas*.

Winter Squash Ice Cream

6 egg yolks
2 cups milk
¾ cup granulated sugar
¼ cup firmly packed brown sugar
Pinch of salt
2 cups heavy (whipping) cream
1 teaspoon vanilla extract
2 cups puréed cooked winter squash
(page 58), from about 1 pound
peeled and cleaned raw squash

Smooth rich ice cream made with puréed pumpkin or other winter squash is fantastic on its own, but for a hedonistic sensation, crown it with toasted pecans, your favorite warmed butterscotch or caramel sauce, and whipped cream.

In the top container of a double boiler off the heat, beat the egg yolks until light and frothy. Add the milk, granulated and brown sugars, and salt and beat until creamy. Place over simmering water in the bottom container of the double boiler and cook, stirring constantly, until the custard coats the back of a metal spoon, about 10 to 15 minutes. Remove from the heat, stir in the cream, vanilla extract, and the squash purée. Cover and refrigerate until very cold, preferably overnight.

Pour into the container of an ice cream maker and freeze according to manufacturer's directions.

Makes about 2 quarts.

Spiced Squash Cake
with Caramel Icing

Preheat an oven to 350° F. Grease and lightly flour a 9-inch bundt pan, or 2 9-inch round cake pans.

To make the cake, sift the flour, baking powder, baking soda, salt, cocoa, cinnamon, ginger, and allspice into a bowl; reserve. In a separate bowl, cream the butter well, add the sugars, and beat until light and fluffy. Add the eggs, one at a time, and beat well. Beat in the vanilla. Fold in about half the reserved dry ingredients, then the buttermilk and pureed squash, and finally the remaining dry ingredients. Stir in the chopped nuts.

Transfer batter to the prepared pan(s) and bake until the cake springs back when touched in the center with a fingertip, about 35 minutes for the bundt pan or 25 minutes for the rounds. Remove pan(s) to a wire rack to cool for 4 or 5 minutes. Turn out onto rack to cool completely.

To make the icing, combine 2½ cups of the sugar and the eggs in a large saucepan and beat with a wire whisk until creamy. Gradually beat in the light cream or half and half. Add the butter, place over medium heat, and bring to a boil, stirring constantly. Meanwhile, place the remaining ½ cup sugar in a heavy skillet over low heat and cook without stirring until the sugar is melted and turns light brown. Immediately pour it into the boiling mixture and continue cooking until the mixture registers 240° F. on a candy thermometer, or until a bit of the mixture dropped into cold water can be gathered into a soft ball. Remove from the heat and cool slightly without stirring, then beat in vanilla.

To glaze the bundt cake as shown, beat the icing just until smooth but still pourable. Quickly spoon it over the cake to coat completely. To use as a spread, beat the mixture until smooth and spreadable, then spread it over the bundt cake, or spread on the top of 1 of the layers, top with the second layer, and ice the top and sides.

Makes 1 9-inch bundt cake, or 1 9-inch two-layer cake; serves 10 to 12.

SPICED SQUASH CAKE
2¼ cups cake flour or unbleached
   all-purpose flour
1 tablespoon baking powder
1 teaspoon baking soda
½ teaspoon salt
1 tablespoon powdered cocoa
2¼ teaspoons ground cinnamon
½ teaspoon ground ginger
½ teaspoon ground allspice
¼ pound (1 stick) unsalted butter,
   softened
½ cup granulated sugar
1 cup firmly packed brown sugar
3 eggs
1 teaspoon vanilla extract
¾ cup buttermilk
¾ cup puréed cooked winter squash
   (page 58), from about 6 ounces
   raw squash
½ cup finely chopped pecans or
walnuts

CARAMEL ICING
3 cups granulated sugar
2 eggs
1⅓ cups light cream or half and half
3 tablespoons unsalted butter
1 teaspoon vanilla extract

Steamed Winter Pudding with Orange Custard Sauce

ORANGE CUSTARD SAUCE
4 egg yolks, at room temperature
½ cup granulated sugar
1¼ cups heavy (whipping) cream
⅓ cup freshly squeezed orange juice
1 tablespoon minced or grated
    orange zest
½ vanilla bean, split, or 1 teaspoon
    vanilla extract

STEAMED WINTER PUDDING
2 cups pureed cooked winter squash
    (page 58), from about 1 pound
    peeled and cleaned raw squash
2 eggs, lightly beaten
1 cup firmly packed light brown
    sugar
¼ pound (1 stick) unsalted butter,
    melted
1 teaspoon vanilla extract
1 teaspoon ground cinnamon
1 teaspoon ground cardamom
¾ teaspoon freshly grated nutmeg
1 teaspoon baking soda
½ teaspoon salt
1½ cups unbleached all-purpose flour
1 cup light cream or half and half

'Buttercup,' 'Butternut,' or 'Sweet Dumpling' squash makes an exceptionally flavorful pudding, as do any of the sweet pumpkins such as 'Small Sugar.' For a festive touch, garnish the pudding with candied orange peel and crystallized violets.

To make the sauce, combine the egg yolks and sugar in the top container of a double boiler off the heat and whisk until light colored, thick, and creamy. Set aside.

Pour the cream into a medium-sized heavy saucepan over medium-high heat and bring almost to a boil. Gradually whisk the cream into the egg yolk mixture. Stir in the orange juice and zest and vanilla bean, if using. Set over simmering water in the bottom of the double boiler and cook, stirring constantly, until the custard is thickened and coats the back of a metal spoon, about 15 minutes. Remove from the heat, cool, and remove vanilla bean, or add vanilla extract, if using. Chill for up to 24 hours before serving.

To make the pudding, combine squash purée, eggs, brown sugar, melted butter, vanilla extract, cinnamon, cardamom, nutmeg, baking soda, salt, flour, and light cream or half and half in a large bowl and stir just enough to mix thoroughly and moisten the flour. Pour into a greased 9-inch round ovenproof mold, cover tightly with a fitted lid or foil, and position on a rack set inside a large pot with a tight fitting lid. Add enough hot, not boiling, water to the pot to come halfway up the sides of the pudding mold. Bring the water to a boil, reduce the heat to simmer, cover the pot, and steam the pudding until set, about 2 to 2½ hours. Alternatively, transfer the covered pot to a preheated 350° F. oven after the water comes to a boil and steam in the oven for about the same amount of time.

Serve the warm pudding with the chilled sauce.

Serves 8.

VARIATION: To bake instead of steam the pudding, pour the mixture into a greased 9-inch round baking pan and bake at 350° F. until set, about 1 hour.

General Index

ACKNOWLEDGMENTS

To Alan May for creating the beautiful and varied works of art used as backgrounds throughout the book.

To Patricia Brabant for once again making magic with her camera. And to her numerous assistants for their great work in the studio and on location in the sweltering summer heat.

To Sharon Silva, one of the best copy editors in the business, for again helping me to sound good.

To the entire staff at Chronicle Books for their continued confidence in my abilities and support of our joint ventures, of which this book makes ten.

To Cleve Gallat, Don Kruse, and Peter Linato of CTA Graphics for their superb typography and mechanical production.

To Marian May for finding photogenic squash in the farmers' markets.

To Mark Carter and everyone at the fabulous Carter House and Hotel Carter in Eureka, California, who made Patricia Brabant, Glen Carroll, and me feel so welcome. Very special thanks to chefs extraordinaire Linda Claasen and Christi Carter for serving great food and sharing recipes.

To Tim Claasen, Ayla Rose and Brad Rother, and Marsha and Richard Daly for letting us photograph and glean from their gardens. And to John and Debbie Salizzoni and Mark Coatec for their terrific hospitality.

To my family and friends who are always so supportive during my intense work periods, especially to Martha and Devereux McNair and John Richardson.

To Addie Prey, Buster Booroo, Michael T. Wigglebut, Joshua J. Chew, and Dweasel Pickle whose companionship was constant throughout this project, even though they don't care very much for squash.

And to my partner Lin Cotton who never fails to contribute good ideas and much-needed encouragement along the way.